Biden-H

Prophecies &

Destruction

Can America survive the next two presidential terms?

Will Joe Biden and Kamala Harris Fulfill Biblical, Islamic, Catholic, Protestant, Hindu, and other America-Related Prophecies?

by Bob Thiel, Ph.D.

www.COGwriter.com

Could the Biden-Harris Administration be apocalyptic?

What is the truth about what will happen in the future?

Edition 1.1 January 2021

Biden-Harris: Prophecies & Destruction

Can America survive the next two presidential terms?

Will Joe Biden and Kamala Harris Fulfill Biblical, Islamic, Catholic, Protestant, Hindu, and other America-Related Prophecies?

by Bob Thiel, Ph.D.

(also known as COGwriter)

Copyright © 2021 by *Nazarene Books*

All rights reserved. No part of this publication may be reproduced, stored in a retrieval system, or transmitted in any means, electronic, mechanical, photocopying, recording, or otherwise without the prior written permission of the copyright holder. Back cover photos of Petra (Jordan) and Dr. Thiel in front of some bricks of the Church of God on Jerusalem's Western Hill, now part of a building known as the Cenacle. Front cover by Nazarene Books. Photos used by permission.

Nazarene Books is wholly owned by Doctors' Research, Inc. Edition 1.0

ISBN 978-1-64106-097-4

Nazarene Books

For those seeking knowledge
www.nazarenebooks.com

CONTENTS

Acknowledgements & Introduction

The author first wishes to thank those who helped him to review this book, which include my wife Joyce and those at Nazarene books.

Scriptural quotes are mainly taken from the *New King James Version* (NKJV) throughout this entire text, unless otherwise noted. Copyright © 1979, 1980, 1982 by Thomas Nelson, Inc. Used by permission. All rights reserved.

The *Douay Rheims Bible* (DRB) is sometimes also used, as it is an old Roman Catholic accepted standard of the Latin Vulgate into the English language. The primary electronic version used here is by permission of William von Peters. The Roman Catholic *New Jerusalem Bible* (NJB) is also sometimes used.

Certain front and back photos are under license or taken by the author's camera. Other photos are public domain as originating from U.S. government sources or granted to the public by the originator.

Introduction and About the Author

The author has studied philosophy, religion, research, science, and prophecy, both formally and informally for several decades. He has multiple degrees, including a Master's degree from the University of Southern California and a Ph.D. from the Union Institute and University. In the past twenty years, the author has had scores of articles published on these topics in a variety of print publications such as magazines, newspapers, and journals. He is also a dedicated Christian and Pastor of the *Continuing* Church of God (official website is www.ccog.org).

Dr. Thiel has been a lifelong researcher and has received several research awards.

He has been married to his wife Joyce since 1981. Together they have made multiple trips to ancient and religious sites in such places as Tikal and Iximche in Guatemala; Ephesus, Smyrna, Pergamos, Thyatira, Sardis, Philadelphia, Laodicea, and Patmos in Asia Minor; Vatican City, Rome, and Pompeii in the Italian peninsula; Athens, Corinth, Crete, and Rhodes in Greece; Fatima in Portugal; and Constantinople (now Istanbul) and Cappadocia in Turkey. They have also visited ancient ruins in Asia, explored parts of Africa and South America, and visited Washington D.C. and most of the states in the U.S.A.

Dr. Thiel is ethnically a Gentile, but strives to spiritually be an Israelite (Galatians 3:29).

The Thiels have three sons and live near the central California coast. The Thiels do not have a worldly political agendum.

Because of his theological interest in both history and prophecy, the author endeavors to make his discoveries available to the public. His writings strive to explain upcoming world events and the peace that is ultimately coming, despite the fact that extremely difficult times are soon ahead. Hundreds of thousands know Dr. Thiel as "COGwriter" and he normally writes three online commentaries daily at the popular www.cogwriter.com website. In addition, he has a YouTube channel titled **BibleNewsProphecy** (www.youtube.com/user/BibleNews Prophecy). The program is also on other platforms such as Vimeo, Brighteon, BitChute, and Dailymotion.

Although this book references a variety of terms, including *saint, blessed, venerable, father, mother, brother, sister, prophet, seer,* etc. to identify writers/sources of predictions, this does not mean that the author agrees that those persons truly held those positions. Those terms mainly are quoted from other sources and/or are included, because they may help in identifying these sources historically.

Also, the term *Roman Catholic* is sometimes used as a distinction from the Eastern Orthodox, the Anglicans, and some others who sometimes use the term *Catholic* to refer to themselves. *Roman* is normally left out when the ties to Rome/Vatican City are obvious by the context, or when something other than the Roman Catholic Church is mentioned.

It should also be understood that the author often comes to different conclusions or interpretations than did some of the reporters/originators of the ancient writings referenced in this book. Readers are encouraged to look up the sources and compare them to the end-time conclusions in this book. Please do not allow traditions or possible written errors to dissuade you from believing the biblical prophecies that will come to pass.

Author's Preface:
Why Bother With Ancient Predictions?

Is the end truly near? Most of us living in these exciting and turbulent times go about our daily activities blissfully or purposely unconcerned about the future. We hear and see reports, through various media, of events converging in ever more intensity on a path toward what? Most don't benefit from an understanding that these events are leading to the fulfillment of many prophecies.

Yet, there are good reasons to "bother" with ancient writings and other sources of prognostication, since we will all be affected by the actions of billions of people who take predictions seriously.

Historically, many powerful civilizations have ultimately been destroyed through economic, military, health and moral decline. Will alliances like NATO remain helpful through these difficulties?

The Bible says not to despise prophecies (1 Thessalonians 5:20). Yet, many people have. We have also seen some past predictions come to pass and some not. Is there a way to understand how today's leaders and the many global alliances are moving toward fulfilling God's Plan? I believe there is and that we have a personal mandate to become aware, involved and prepared!

While I believe that it is the Bible which is Divinely inspired (2 Timothy 3:16), I invite you on a journey of discovery that will look at other-sourced prophecies as well: Islam, Hindu, Native American, Catholic, New Age, etc. as many will be affected by them. Relating to, and/or citing, cultural writings of others is a long-used technique in even biblical communications (e.g. Acts 17:23, 28; 1 Corinthians 9:20-22).

We are all affected by leaders who act according to their religious and other beliefs.

Did you know that people of various faiths, like Christian, Catholic, Hopi, Hindu, and Buddhism are eagerly anticipating a new age of peace to dawn soon? Some expect this will be a golden age of peace while others believe it will only come about by the emergence of a single and/or inter-faith religion. Did you know that the Vatican and the United Nations are working hard toward this goal?

At least a dozen predictions in my book about Barack Obama came to pass as did at least twenty related to Donald Trump in my book about him.

The Bible itself predicts an age of peace (the millennial Kingdom of God), but it shows that a horrible, militaristic dictator will first appear and implement a type of false ecumenical religion while enforcing a militaristic "peace" upon the world. The entire world faces enormous challenges ahead. Even respected scientists are verifying that bizarre occurrences are expected.

I wrote this book in the hope that you would like to discover what things must, and may soon, come to pass, and some ways in which Joe Biden and/or Kamala Harris may be involved. If you will properly heed them, I believe the decisions you make based on these predictions could actually save your life and the lives of those you love.

Bob Thiel, Ph.D.

1. Joe Biden: Background, Controversies, and Hebrew Prophecy

We are living in perilous times (2 Timothy 3:1-5). Partially because of this, Joe Biden and Kamala Harris were elected to be the President and Vice-President of the United States.

Joe Biden was born on November 20, 1942 in Scranton, Pennsylvania. His full birth name was Joseph Robinette Biden, Jr. His parents were Joseph Robinette Biden, Sr. and Catherine Eugenia (Finnegan) Biden. The Bidens had four children, with Joe, Jr. the oldest.

Joseph, Sr. had been wealthy, but lost much of his wealth by the time of his first child's birth. Joe, Sr. later became a successful used car salesman.

The Bidens were Roman Catholic family and Joe Biden asserts he follows that religion to this day.

Joe Biden attended St. Paul's Elementary School in Scranton. In 1955, the family moved to Mayfield, Delaware. Joe Biden attended the St. Helena School until he gained acceptance into the prestigious Archmere Academy. There he played football as a receiver. He graduated from Archmere in 1961.

Although Joe Biden graduated from various universities, he made exaggerated claims about how good a student he was, that were not true.[1] Furthermore, "he graduated 76th out of a law school class of 85. His undergraduate academic records show that he graduated from {the University of} Delaware 506th in a class of 688 with a 'C' average and that he got his undergraduate degree with a dual major in history and political science." [2] "Biden was at best a mediocre law student."[3]

Joe Biden, age 10

On August 27, 1966, Joe Biden married a non-Roman Catholic named Neilia Hunter. They had three children: Joseph R. "Beau" Biden III (1969–2015), Robert Hunter Biden (born 1970), and Naomi Christina "Amy" Biden (1971–1972). [4]

In 1969, Joe Biden practiced law as a public defender. After becoming an active member in the Democratic Party, he was elected to the New Castle County Council in 1971. [5] In 1972, after an election with a large turnout, Biden won and became the fifth-youngest U.S. senator elected in the nation's history. [6]

His wife Neila and daughter Naomi died in an automobile accident in December 1972.

He later married teacher Jill Tracy Jacobs at the United Nations chapel in New York on June 17, 1977. They had a daughter together, Ashley Blazer, who was born 1981.

"In 1987, having established himself as one of Washington's most prominent Democratic lawmakers, Biden decided to run for the U.S. presidency. He dropped out of the Democratic primary, however, after reports surfaced that he had plagiarized part of a speech." [7]

In 2008, he ran for vice president under Barack Obama. On January 20, 2009, Joe Biden became the 47th vice president of the U.S.

Joe Biden tends to be ecumenical:

> [I]n 2009, ... Biden had warmly referred to the personality, ministry and initiatives of the Ecumenical Patriarch, for promoting interfaith dialogue, [8]

Some world leaders have put their hopes in the ecumenical and interfaith movements tied to the Church of Rome to solve humanities ills — biblically this is warned against (cf. 2 Corinthians 6:17; Revelation 17; see also the free booklet, *The Gospel of the Kingdom of God*, available in over 100 languages at ccog.org for more details).

Joe Biden, himself, has been accused, on numerous occasions of inappropriate touching and making inappropriate comments to women (including fairly young ones). It has been claimed that this was a major reason he did not run for president in 2016. [9]

Getting back to the Biden family, Joe's brother James/Jim and Joe's son Hunter have essentially been accused of influence peddling and profiting off of Joe's political position(s) relating to Ukraine and China. Emails provided evidence:

> The Biden emails exhibits what was lengthy abundantly clear that Hunter Biden and his uncle engaged in a worldwide affect peddling scheme. There is now a federal legal investigation and witness testimony straight contradicting the statements of Joe Biden. [10]

The US Federal Bureau of Investigation has been involved and we will see what, if anything, the courts decide about this.

End-Time Leaders and Prophecy

The focus of this book is on biblical prophecies and how the Biden-Harris Administration may be involved in events leading to the fulfillment of them, including those that show the coming destruction of the United States.

There are prophecies from several sources that warn against leaders and various actions in the days leading up to the Great Tribulation, often called the 'Apocalypse.'

The Bible itself warns that if the children of Israel sinned and did not repent, the following would happen:

> [12] ... Those who lead you cause you to err, And destroy the way of your paths. (Isaiah 3:12)

> [16] For the leaders of this people cause them to err, And those who are led by them are destroyed. (Isaiah 9:16)

Since multiple millions of the physical descendants of Israel reside in the United States and we are getting close to the end, it is interesting to note that the above prophecies have been fulfilled, to a degree, during administrations of recent U.S. presidents (with issues such as debt), and potentially will also be fulfilled during a Biden-Harris Administration. Those who are not physical descendants, but reside in the U.S.A., also will be affected by the same biblical prophecies (cf. Numbers 25:16).

Joe Biden: Some Additional Background and Prophetic Connections

Joe Biden's mother was of Irish descent and Joseph, Sr. had English, French, and Irish ancestry. This heritage is of interest biblically.

The Bible shows that Isaac's son Jacob was renamed Israel by God (Genesis 32:28). Israel had twelve sons, which ended up becoming thirteen tribes (the descendants of Joseph became two tribes). The term 'Saxon' has long been believed by some to be a derivative of the expression "Isaac's son' and that the term Scot is also a derivative of that and/or the term Scythian (cf. Colossians 3:11).[11] (Many scholars say that the term Scot came from the Latin word *scotus*, but do not know where that came from.)

What many seem to fail to realize is that the nation currently called Israel, along with the Jews scattered around the world, does not represent all the "children of Israel."

The Jews were named for being the descendants of Israel's son Judah. The Bible shows that there was a split between the supporters of Judah and the other tribes after the death of King Solomon (1 Kings 12:16-20). Most of the descendants of Israel were not Jews.

Ten of the tribes were given to a leader named Jeroboam (1 Kings 11:31) and were then known as the kingdom of Israel. The capital of Israel was in the territory of Manasseh and was called Samaria (1 Kings 16:24-29). The Bible sometimes uses the term Samaria when referring to those of Manasseh (Isaiah 9:8-21; Hosea 7:1; 10:1-11; Amos 3:12; 6:1; Obadiah 1:19). Many prophecies in the Bible related to Israel and/or Samaria are not necessarily for, nor limited to, people of Jewish heritage (cf. 1 Kings 16:2; Isaiah 3:12; 9:8-12,21; Hosea 7:1). The Bible also uses the term 'Samaria' to distinguish between the descendants of Israel who are Jewish and those descendants of Israel who are not Jewish (cf. Isaiah 10:10-11; Ezekiel 16:1,46, 23:4; Micah 1:1-6). Jewish scholars realize that the Bible shows that Samaria consisted of an ethnic mix of Israelites and non-Israelites.[12]

A reading of the Book of Genesis shows that Israel specifically placed his name on the two sons of Joseph named Ephraim and Manasseh (Genesis 48:14-16), neither of which were Jewish. Israel also had other sons, like Dan and Reuben some of whose descendants ended up in Ireland and France respectively.

What does any of this have to do with Joe Biden?

Well as it turns out, since everyone had to descend from someone, ultimately their progenitors are somewhere listed in the Bible. Hence, biblical writings and prophecies can often be tied to descendants of those progenitors the Bible discusses.

Certain Jewish sages and others have recognized that the British peoples descended from the tribe of Ephraim.[13] Some also felt that by the time the U.S.A. formed, a high amount of the people who went to the land that the U.S.A. dominates had descended from the ancient tribe of Manasseh.[14]

In the case of Joe Biden, it looks like he is primarily, ethnically, an Israelite. The nation he is to lead, while an ethnic mixture bringing to mind biblical Samaria, is on the receiving side of the end-time prophecies related to Joseph's son Manasseh.

Joseph's Descendants

The Bible records the promise from Israel that Ephraim would become a group of nations and that Manasseh would become an important nation on its own. At least one Jewish scholar interpreted certain passages of scripture to mean that Ephraim would rise up first and that Manasseh would rise up later.[15]

After the rise of the British Empire, some people started to wonder if the British were the people of the covenant promises to Ephraim. A few Christians, Jews, and others began to write about this, as well as the rising up of the U.S. as a major power, in the 19th, 20th, and 21st centuries.[16]

Interestingly, the Hebrew term often translated as "covenant" in Isaiah and elsewhere in the Old Testament is *beriyth*[17] and the word for "man" is *iysh*[18] (found in Isaiah 46:8). Together those words are pronounced similar to the term "British."

In the Bible, the descendants of Joseph's sons (Genesis 49:22-26) were promised prosperity and blessings, which the U.S.A. and its Anglo-Saxon descended allies have enjoyed. Yet, Jesus warned that "to whom much is given" from such "much will be required" (Luke 12:48). And the Bible also warns of curses for those who forsake God's laws (Deuteronomy 28:15-57). So, blessings and cursings are in prophecies.

Without going into all the historical details here (many of which can be found in the article *Anglo - America in Prophecy*

15

& the Lost Tribes of Israel, available at the www.cogwriter.com website), the connection with Mr. Biden's heritage is of interest. Various prophecies related to the end-time descendants of Isaac's sons are included in this book.

A 9/11 Prophecy? Foreign Policy?

Joe Biden falsely claimed that he predicted the 9/11 attack the day before it happened:

> Joe Biden for years falsely claimed in interviews that he predicted the 9/11 terror attacks and a possible strike on the White House in a speech delivered the day before terrorists flew planes into the Twin Towers. ... when al Qaeda terrorists hijacked four planes the following morning and killed 2,977 Americans, Biden began claiming he predicted the attack.
>
> He did no such thing. During the hour-long speech, Biden mentioned terrorism only three times — twice in reference to biological terrorism.
>
> But in an interview with ABC News just hours after the Twin Towers fell, Biden, then chairman of the Senate Foreign Relations Committee, said he warned that planes could be hijacked and flown into buildings like the White House.
>
> "Literally as recently as yesterday, I spoke to the National Press Club and talked about the fact that it is just as easy to fly from National Airport into the White House as it is to, you know, do the same thing in New York," Biden said.
>
> "On Sept. 10, the day before the attacks on the towers, I made a speech to the National Press Club

16

where I warned about a massive attack on the United States of America from terrorists, why I thought it would happen and why I thought our priorities were misplaced — the day before 9/11," Biden said on the Senate floor in 2006. ...

Biden's history of making revisionist remarks has also come under fire after he claimed on last year's primary campaign trail that he was opposed to the Iraq War, which he voted for — drawing the ire of primary opponent Bernie Sanders.[19]

Joe Biden has a history of making inaccurate statements about himself.

It has been suggested that the following is a prophecy related to the terrorist attacks of 9/11/2001:[20]

9 All the people will know — Ephraim and the inhabitant of Samaria — Who say in pride and arrogance of heart: 10 'The bricks have fallen down, But we will rebuild with hewn stones; The sycamores are cut down, But we will replace them with cedars." (Isaiah 9:9-10)

Essentially the leaders of ancient Ephraim and Manasseh declared that they would rebuild. A few prophecy-watchers have stated that Isaiah 9:9-10 seems to be related to what happened in the U.S.A. because of the 9/11/2001 attacks.

At a memorial ceremony for it, Joe Biden stated, "We come not to mourn but to remember and rebuild." [21]

At least one prophecy-watcher has believed that American politicians making "rebuild" statements" were taking *defiance* types of positions that Isaiah warned against.[22] Like ancient Ephraim and Manasseh, God was left out of the equation.

Since certain prophecies about Samaria appear to be directed towards the U.S.A. of the 21st century (e.g. Isaiah 10:4-11; Hosea 7:1-3), and this makes those ties to Isaiah 9 potentially stronger.

Presuming that end-time Samaria ties with Manasseh AND Isaiah 9:9-10 has an end-time fulfillment, then Joe Biden has been one of several leaders to at least partially fulfill this by pridefully boasting that a more majestic rebuilding will occur because of human effort.

As far as foreign policy goes, former Defense Secretary Robert Gates wrote that Joe Biden "had been wrong on nearly every major foreign policy and national security issues over the past four decades." [23] If that has much truth to it, then a Joe Biden foreign policy will be disastrous.

As far as internal policy goes, Joe Biden has claimed, on many occasions, that he was the original author of the so-called Patriot Act, as he wrote a version of it in 1994. [24] The Patriot Act is a law that has resulted in increased surveillance and loss of civil liberties in the U.S.A. Furthermore, as even Joe Biden admits, "Civil libertarians were opposed to it" [25] (it being what he introduced back in 1994). Joe Biden has a history of wanting more government controls.

Furthermore, consider that Joe Biden said those who protested his election and stormed the Capitol in January 2021 were "domestic terrorists" and that he wants another law:

> "Don't dare call them protesters," Mr. Biden said in remarks from Wilmington, Del. "They were a riotous mob. Insurrectionists. Domestic terrorists. It's that basic. It's that simple." … Mr. Biden has said he

plans to make a priority of passing a law against domestic terrorism … [26]

Such a law will lead to more surveillance, restrictions, and basically more totalitarian controls. While the violence associated with the storming of the Capitol should be condemned, Joe Biden and Kamala Harris did not show the same attitude (calling them "domestic terrorists) towards those who rioted, looted, and burned buildings during 2020 protests.

If the following biblical prophecy has an end-time fulfillment, it seems to suggest that a male leader will be in charge when the U.S.A. falls:

> [7] As for Samaria, her king is cut off Like a twig on the water. [8] Also the high places of Aven, the sin of Israel, Shall be destroyed. The thorn and thistle shall grow on their altars; They shall say to the mountains, "Cover us!" And to the hills, "Fall on us!" … [10] When it is My desire, I will chasten them. Peoples shall be gathered against them When I bind them for their two transgressions. (Hosea 10:7,8,10)

If Hosea 10:7-10 has end-time connotations (and part of it seems to, cf. Revelation 6:16), AND presuming that the Hebrew word translated as "king" literally means a male, then it might be possible that Joe Biden could be the last President/leader of the United States. However, someone else could be the last as the year when the disaster in Hosea 10:7 would be fulfilled is not currently clear, nor do I believe it can happen prior to 2024. Plus, it is not clear that Joe Biden will actually remain in office, because of his age, physical, and mental health.

The 46th President of the United States

The Electoral College declared that Joe Biden was elected as the 46th president of the United States. Here is what the Biden-Harris Administration's top priority is:

> The Equality Act is the best vehicle for ensuring equal rights under the law for LGBTQ+ Americans, and will guarantee that LGBTQ+ individuals are protected under existing civil rights laws. **Biden will make enactment of the Equality Act during his first 100 days as President a top legislative priority**. Biden will also direct his Cabinet to ensure immediate and full enforcement of the Equality Act across all federal departments and agencies. ... **End the misuse of broad exemptions to discriminate.** Religious freedom is a fundamental American value. But states have inappropriately used broad exemptions to allow businesses, medical providers, social service agencies, state and local government officials, and others to discriminate against LGBTQ+ people. **Guaranteeing transgender students have access to facilities based on their gender identity...** Biden will reverse Trump's policies misusing these broad exemptions and fight so that no one is turned away from a business or refused service by a government official just because of who they are or who they love. [27]

The above is a concern to many people who believe that they will be discriminated against if they hold to various religious and/or biblical beliefs on sexuality. Claiming religious freedom is "a fundamental American value" (which is clearly stated in the U.S. Constitution) while at the same time saying it must be not allowed for certain matters is wrong, insincere, and hypocritical.

The Bible, KJV translation, predicts the end of "an hypocritical nation" (Isaiah 10:5-11).

That being said, despite the Biden-Harris priorities and what has so far happened with matters like COVID-19, I can state with biblical assurance that the time that the Bible calls the "Great Tribulation" (Matthew 24:21) will NOT begin until sometime after the first presidential term of Joe Biden ends.

However, the end of the 6,000 years God has granted humanity to rule itself will likely be over within the next decade or so (some details are in Chapter 6 and a more detailed discussion of this is in an article at the website www.cogwriter.com). Thus, simply by the virtue of timing, Joe Biden is destined to take steps that ultimately will aid in the fulfillment of end-time biblical prophecies. Furthermore, several of the stated policies for the Biden-Harris Administration have biblical ramifications.

For example, as president, Joe Biden will have to deal with the fact that the U.S.A. is the most indebted nation in the history of humanity. Plus, he has pledged increasing it further. [28]

Debt is a prophesied problem (cf. Habakkuk 2:6-8). But many in the media as well as politically-inclined economists do not see it that way—but that is too short sighted (cf. Ecclesiastes 8:11).

The time will come when the U.S.A. government will no longer be able to borrow at low interest rates and/or it will create more money electronically and/or via the printing press to try to continue.

Make no mistake about it -- massive inflation is coming.

The U.S.A. dollar will ultimately crash and be worthless. That "pride" of American power will be broken (cf. Leviticus 26:19).

A Biden-Harris Administration has asserted it will take debt raising steps.

A Short Term for Joe Biden?

In October of 2020 Speaker of the House Nancy Pelosi proposed changes to the 25th Amendment to the US Constitution to make it easier for Congress to remove a president. if the president was incapable of the job. Some suspect, because of Joe Biden's health and age, this was done to help pave the way for a Kamala Harris presidency.

Speaker Pelosi said the proposal was NOT directed towards Donald Trump, who then made the following statements about it:

> Nancy Pelosi is looking at the 25th Amendment in order to replace Joe Biden with Kamala Harris … The Dems want that to happen fast because Sleepy Joe is out of it!!! … this 25th Amendment, I think they put it in so they can get Kamala in." [29]

I expect that Kamala Harris will either be the *de facto* president, possibly being the actual president of the U.S.A. as Joe Biden has issues that will lead to that.

2. Kamala Harris Background, Immorality, and Prophetic Consequences

Kamala Devi Harris was born in Oakland, California on October 20, 1964.

"Kamala means 'lotus' and is another name for the Hindu goddess Lakshmi—and the empowerment of women."[30] Kamala means lotus flower in Sanskrit. Whereas Devi is the Hindu deity also known as Mahadevi or 'Great Goddess,' the all-embracing Mother Goddess. [31]

Kamala Harris' mother, Shyamala Gopalan, was a biologist from Tamil, India. Her father, Donald J. Harris, who became an economics professor at Stanford University, came to the U.S.A. from Jamaica. He and his parents are considered to have "Afro-Jamaican heritage," which seems to be mainly a combination of British and African heritage.

Kamala's parents divorced when she was 7. At age 12, she moved with her mother and sister to Quebec. She attended Westmount High School in Quebec, where she founded a dance troupe with a friend. Kamala later attended Howard University in Washington, D.C., where she earned a B.A. in political science and economics. Kamala Harris then enrolled at the University of California, Hastings College of the Law, earning her J.D. in 1989. [32]

Although 50% of people who take the California Bar exam pass on their first attempt, Kamala Harris did not. [33]

After she finally passed, Harris began her career as a deputy district attorney in Alameda County.

She later connected with a very powerful California politician named Willie Brown:

In 1994, Harris began dating Willie Brown, a powerhouse in California politics who was then the speaker of the state assembly and was 30 years older than Harris. From his perch in the assembly, Brown appointed Harris to the California Unemployment Insurance Appeals Board and the Medical Assistance Commission—positions that together paid her around $80,000 a year on top of her prosecutor's salary.[34]

Willie Brown, ... 60 year old and "his 29 year old mistress, Kamala." ... Brown was legally married at the time. [35]

It appears obvious that her adulterous affair with a legally married and influential man assisted her career advancement. The view of comedienne Roseann Barr was that Kamala Harris "slept her way to the bottom" to get her political career going. [36]

Later, as attorney general Kamala Harris "made waves for her refusal to defend Proposition 8, a 2008 California ballot measure" that defined marriage as between a male and female. [37] Of course, that is also how Jesus defined marriage (cf. Matthew 19:4-5).

Kamala "Harris married lawyer Doug Emhoff on August 22, 2014, in Santa Barbara, California. She is the stepmother of his two children, Ella and Cole." [38] Her husband is Jewish.

In November 2016, she was elected to the US Senate.

In her 2019 book, *The Truths We Hold: An American Journey*, she has the following statement:

There, my earliest memories of the Bible's teachings were of a loving God, a God who asked us "to speak up for those who cannot speak for themselves" and to defend the rights of the poor and needy." [39]

Beyond that, there do not seem to be many truths Kamala Harris holds related to scripture. And for those of us who believe our religious rights are needy in the 21st century, she along with Joe Biden has essentially stated that we must expect that the rights of those with certain differing views on sexuality surpass our own. Hence, from the perspective of a religious minority, it does not seem she takes such defense seriously.

There are reports that as an adult Kamala Harris claimed to have fallen from a stroller as a toddler at a protest rally and then said she wanted "fweedom" ("it turns out Kamala Harris lifted her "Fweedom" story from a 1965 Playboy interview with Martin Luther King, by Alex Haley") and that she celebrated Kwanza before it was likely possible as it was a holiday invented in 1966. [40] So, some have questioned aspects of her childhood memories.

"Kamala Harris, … attended services at both a Black Baptist church and a Hindu temple growing up – an interfaith background." [41] She now asserts she is a Baptist, holding membership at the Third Baptist Church of San Francisco.

Kamala Harris Prophecies?

Unlike Joe Biden, Kamala Harris is predominantly of Gentile heritage (as is this author).

The Bible teaches the following:

[43] The alien who is among you shall rise higher and

higher above you, and you shall come down lower and lower (Deuteronomy 28:43).

Having a Kamala Harris vice-president, along with many race-specific Biden-Harris plans for the U.S.A. listed at the official JoeBiden.com website, [42] look to promote those that ethnically are not primarily of Israelite heritage. The bias of these policies towards those the Biden-Harris plan calls "Black and Brown Americans" [43] may further increase the divide in the U.S.A. Some expect a "white awakening" that may oppose aspects of that agenda. [44]

Jesus, Himself, predicted:

> [7] For there will be an intifada of ethnic group against ethnic group, (Matthew 24:7a, Orthodox Jewish Bible)

> [17] … Every kingdom divided against itself is brought to desolation, and a house divided against a house falls. (Luke 11:17b, NKJV)

"Intifada" essentially means rebellion or uprising. We have seen that in protests and riots in the past, and a Biden-Harris Administration looks to trigger racial protests. Further dividing of the U.S.A. will not end well.

Speaking of division, as of January 15, 2021, it looks like the U.S. Senate will be divided essentially in half, in terms of Republicans and Democrats (technically Bernie Sanders is an independent, but can usually be relied on to support the Democrats). As vice-president, Kamala Harris will be able to cast any needed tie-breaking vote in the Senate, hence she is set to become a very powerful person.

Kamala Harris is also female and looks to be one who is fulfilling the following prophecy in these end times:

[12] As for My people, children are their oppressors, And women rule over them. O My people! Those who lead you cause you to err, And destroy the way of your paths. (Isaiah 3:12)

While certainly there are places for women (Judges chapters 4 & 5) and Gentiles (2 Chronicles 36:22) in leadership positions, Isaiah does not suggest that this should be looked at as a great blessing.

Since the time of Margaret Thatcher, I have felt that it is likely that the U.S.A. would end up with a female president or at least a highly influential woman in a top level federal government job. As it turns out, the four remaining predominantly British-descended nations (the United Kingdom, Canada, Australia, and New Zealand) all have had not only queens (they shared the same ones), but all have already had a woman in the office of prime minister. The prime minister is the chief executive official in a parliamentary system of governance.

While a female U.S. president is not strictly required per Isaiah 3:12, one should be considered likely.

Immorality

As a non-partisan, it is sometimes difficult to write certain parts of this book as some people are bound to believe that I am intentionally taking a partisan stance.

I am not.

I am not a Republican nor a Democrat nor part of any political party. Nor do I consider myself an independent or some type of anarchist. My views would be that of a biblical Christian who earnestly holds to true and original Christian beliefs (cf. Jude 3).

(Perhaps it should be mentioned that when Donald Trump was President of the United States, I also had a book about him,[45] and at least 20 predictions I published related to him and his Administration came to pass.)

While I wish that the future of the United States in the next decade or so would be its greatest years, the moral direction that the U.S. has taken, along with various statements in the Bible, point to the fact that we are getting closer to the end of America.

It is reasonable to believe that not everything that a Biden-Harris Administration may do will be good, and not all that Administration may do will be bad. The same goes for other political leaders.

Regarding Biden-Harris views on abortion, notice the following items:

> Biden will work to codify Roe v. Wade, and his Justice Department will do everything in its power to stop the rash of state laws that so blatantly violate *Roe v. Wade*. Restore federal funding for Planned Parenthood. … Restore the Affordable Care Act's contraception mandate in place before the U.S. Supreme Court's Hobby Lobby decision. [46]

> Pro-life leaders have warned against Joe Biden's "aggressively pro-abortion" pick to lead the Department of Health and Human Services. California Attorney General Xavier Becerra has a long track record in taking legal action against pro-life organizations. [47]

> Harris is so pro-abortion that serving in the Senate, she has maintained a 100% rating from the pro-

abortion rights group National Association for the Repeal of Abortion Laws (NARAL). [48]

Here is information on the Biden-Harris LGBTQ plans:

> As President, Biden will restore the United States' standing as a global leader defending LGBTQ+ rights and development … [49]

> As President, Biden will … Decriminalize HIV exposure and transmission laws … ban so-called "conversion therapy." [50]

The Bible says that those who were homosexual can change (1 Corinthians 6:9-11), and the first amendment of the U.S. Constitution supposedly guarantees the right of free assembly. So how any government in the U.S.A. can outlaw "conversion therapy" shows that the U.S.A. has declined deeply in this area.

Many have questioned Joe Biden's and Kamala Harris' morality. From their pro-abortion positions to their plan to globally promote the LGBTQ+ agenda while restricting religious rights of those who have differing standards, these would biblically be considered as noticeable moral flaws.

Notice also the following:

> President-elect Joe Biden's transition team leader for US-owned media outlets wants to redefine freedom of speech and make "hate speech" a crime. Richard Stengel is the Biden transition "Team Lead" for the US Agency for Global Media …

> "In general, hate speech is speech that attacks and insults people on the basis of race, religion, ethnic origin and sexual orientation," Stengel wrote. [51]

Does any of that matter? Global media, 'big tech,' and many governments have already censored scriptures (and even I have been directly censored by Vimeo, at least once, for tying certain world events in with biblical prophecies).

Notice also some of what the Bible says and it teaches:

> [8] Now go, write it before them on a tablet, And note it on a scroll, That it may be for time to come, Forever and ever:
>
> [9] That this is a rebellious people, Lying children, Children who will not hear the law of the Lord;
>
> [10] Who say to the seers, "Do not see,"
>
> And to the prophets, "Do not prophesy to us right things; Speak to us smooth things, prophesy deceits. [11] Get out of the way, Turn aside from the path, Cause the Holy One of Israel To cease from before us." (Isaiah 30:8-11)
>
> [20] Woe to those who call evil good, and good evil; Who put darkness for light, and light for darkness; Who put bitter for sweet, and sweet for bitter! [21] Woe to those who are wise in their own eyes, And prudent in their own sight! (Isaiah 5:20-21)
>
> [1] Cry aloud, spare not; Lift up your voice like a trumpet; Tell My people their transgression, And the house of Jacob their sins. (Isaiah 58:1)

More and more people do not want to hear the truths related to the law of God or prophecies from His word.

Consider also that if some are insulted because their sins are called out, at least some associated with the Biden-Harris team want to make that a crime!

Yes, various ones want to further stifle religious speech to the point of persecuting those who hold to aspects of biblical morality.

Like certain others, Joe Biden and Kamala Harris are helping to fulfill the following prophecy for the "last days":

> [1] But know this, that **in the last days** perilous times will come: [2] For **men will be lovers of themselves, lovers of money, boasters, proud, blasphemers**, disobedient to parents, unthankful, unholy, [3] unloving, unforgiving, **slanderers, without self-control, brutal, despisers of good**, [4] traitors, **headstrong, haughty**, lovers of pleasure rather than lovers of God, [5] having a form of godliness but denying its power. And **from such people turn away!** [6] For of this sort are those who creep into households and make captives of gullible women loaded down with sins, led away by various lusts, [7] **always learning and never able to come to the knowledge of the truth**. (2 Timothy 3:1-7)

Proud, boasters, lovers of themselves, and headstrong; if you do not believe these terms help describe people like the Biden-Harris teams, consider that they push "pride" events and have asserted that religious rights need to be scaled back.

Is that not headstrong and haughty?

Kamala Harris is an admitted adulterer. She and Joe Biden claim Christianity but certainly do not promote all aspects of biblical morality.

With debt and rising public immorality, the United States has been setting the stage for the type of death/devastation that the Apostle Paul warned about:

31

[22] Professing to be wise, they became fools, ...

[26] For this reason God gave them up to vile passions. For even their women exchanged the natural use for what is against nature. [27] Likewise also the men, leaving the natural use of the woman, burned in their lust for one another, men with men committing what is shameful, and receiving in themselves the penalty of their error which was due.

[28] And even as they did not like to retain God in their knowledge, God gave them over to a debased mind, to do those things which are not fitting; [29] being filled with all unrighteousness, sexual immorality, wickedness, covetousness, maliciousness; full of envy, murder, strife, deceit, evil-mindedness; they are whisperers, [30] backbiters, haters of God, violent, proud, boasters, inventors of evil things, disobedient to parents, [31] undiscerning, untrustworthy, unloving, unforgiving, unmerciful; [32] who, knowing the righteous judgment of God, that **those who practice such things are deserving of death, not only do the same but also approve of those who practice them.** (Romans 1:26-32)

The above scriptures are clearly condemning covetousness, sexual immorality, and that even approving of them leads to death. And many others in the U.S.A. participate in or at least seemingly approve of many of these sins.

These are factors that will lead to the death and destruction of the United States.

While this author has major theological issues with Franklin Graham (son of the late Billy Graham), notice what Franklin Graham said on January 6, 2021:

After the election of Joe Biden, who supports the killing of the unborn almost without limit, voters in Georgia apparently have given two Senate seats to Democrats who are part of a "demonic-driven abortion agenda," says evangelist Franklin Graham.

"We are in trouble" he said. "I believe God's judgment is coming, for the sins of our nation are great and they are a stench in the nostrils of our Creator." [52]

Yes, God's judgment is coming to the U.S.A.

Notice also:

> [22] Therefore say to the house of Israel, "Thus says the Lord God: "I do not do this for your sake, O house of Israel, but for My holy name's sake, which you have profaned among the nations wherever you went. [23] And I will sanctify My great name, which has been profaned among the nations, which you have profaned in their midst; and the nations shall know that I am the Lord," says the Lord God, "when I am hallowed in you before their eyes. [24] For I will take you from among the nations, gather you out of all countries, and bring you into your own land. [25] Then I will sprinkle clean water on you, and you shall be clean; I will cleanse you from all your filthiness and from all your idols." (Ezekiel 36:22-25)

Furthermore, understand that the Bible specifically teaches that various forms of sexual immorality defile a nation:

> [22] You shall not lie with a male as with a woman. It is an abomination. [23] Nor shall you mate with any animal, to defile yourself with it. Nor shall any woman stand before an animal to mate with it. It is perversion.

²⁴ 'Do not defile yourselves with any of these things; for by all these the nations are defiled, which I am casting out before you. ²⁵ For the land is defiled; therefore I visit the punishment of its iniquity upon it, and the land vomits out its inhabitants. ²⁶ You shall therefore keep My statutes and My judgments, and shall not commit any of these abominations, either any of your own nation or any stranger who dwells among you ²⁷ (for all these abominations the men of the land have done, who were before you, and thus the land is defiled), ²⁸ lest the land vomit you out also when you defile it, as it vomited out the nations that were before you. ²⁹ For whoever commits any of these abominations, the persons who commit them shall be cut off from among their people. (Leviticus 18:22-29)

⁵ For this you know, that no fornicator, unclean person, nor covetous man, who is an idolater, has any inheritance in the kingdom of Christ and God. ⁶ Let no one deceive you with empty words, for because of these things the wrath of God comes upon the sons of disobedience. (Ephesians 5:5-6)

Some believe scripture, others will not.

Weather Prophecies

The Bible ties weather blessings in with morality:

³ 'If you walk in My statutes and keep My commandments, and perform them, ⁴ then I will give you rain in its season, the land shall yield its produce, and the trees of the field shall yield their fruit. ⁵ Your threshing shall last till the time of vintage, and the vintage shall last till the time of

sowing; you shall eat your bread to the full and dwell in your land safely. (Leviticus 26:3-5)

Yet, the promotion of more and more aspects of immorality will lead to the destruction of the U.S.A. (cf. Isaiah 1:28; Hosea 7:13), and may also cause weather problems.

Notice some of how the Bible ties weather in with sins:

[15] "But it shall come to pass, if you do not obey the voice of the Lord your God, to observe carefully all His commandments and His statutes which I command you today, that all these curses will come upon you and overtake you: ... [22] The Lord will strike you with consumption, with fever, with inflammation, with severe burning fever, with the sword, with scorching, and with mildew; they shall pursue you until you perish. [23] And your heavens which are over your head shall be bronze, and the earth which is under you shall be iron. [24] The Lord will change the rain of your land to powder and dust; from the heaven it shall come down on you until you are destroyed. (Deuteronomy 28:15-24)

[1] The word of the Lord that came to Jeremiah concerning the droughts. ... [7] O Lord, though our iniquities testify against us, ... For our backslidings are many, We have sinned against You. (Jeremiah 14:1-7)

[6] "Also I gave you cleanness of teeth in all your cities. And lack of bread in all your places; Yet you have not returned to Me, "Says the Lord. [7] I also withheld rain from you, When there were still three months to the harvest. I made it rain on one city, I withheld rain from another city. One part was rained upon, And where it did not rain the part withered. [8]

So two or three cities wandered to another city to drink water, But they were not satisfied; Yet you have not returned to Me, "Says the Lord.

9 "I blasted you with blight and mildew. When your gardens increased, Your vineyards, Your fig trees, And your olive trees, The locust devoured them; Yet you have not returned to Me, "Says the Lord. …

11 "I overthrew some of you, As God overthrew Sodom and Gomorrah, And you were like a firebrand plucked from the burning; Yet you have not returned to Me, "Says the Lord.

12 "Therefore thus will I do to you, O Israel; Because I will do this to you, Prepare to meet your God, O Israel!" (cf. Amos 4:6-9, 11-12).

Many feel that weather is purely random, but the Bible teaches that God controls the weather (Psalm 148:8) and sometimes provides extreme weather because of human sins to encourage people to repent. Weather issues will contribute to pestilences (Amos 4:9; cf. Matthew 24:7).

Notice what is also prophesied to happen to end-time Babylon:

38 A drought is against her waters, and they will be dried up. For it is the land of carved images, And they are insane with their idols. 39 "Therefore the wild desert beasts shall dwell there with the jackals, And the ostriches shall dwell in it. It shall be inhabited no more forever, Nor shall it be dwelt in from generation to generation. 40 As God overthrew Sodom and Gomorrah And their neighbors," says the Lord, "So no one shall reside there, Nor son of man dwell in it. (Jeremiah 50:38-40)

So, both Amos and Jeremiah tied the warning of a drought in with later being overthrown like Sodom and Gomorrah.

The Bible says that Sodom and Gomorrah were overthrown as examples for those who would go after "strange flesh" (2 Peter 2:6).

The following was in a book I wrote and published back in 2009 related to expect prophetic events:

Odd weather patterns result in food shortages and natural disasters.	Matthew 24:7
The world is actually in a berserk transition, as the real age of peace is not yet here. It may be a period of chaos. It is the beginning of sorrows.	Matthew 24:8

This has begun to happen. Record heat and odd weather have occurred.[53]

These problems should serve as a wake-up call. Increased acceptance of immorality is associated with weather problems in the Bible in many places (e.g. Deuteronomy 28:15-24; Amos 4:6-12).

Unless there is national repentance, a Biden-Harris Administration will not positively change the true moral direction of the U.S.A. There will be more odd and berserk weather.

Dealing with "fossil fuels," without dealing with sins will not stop a coming massive heat—particularly the one that happens after the U.S.A. is no more (Revelation 16:9).

A Roman Catholic Prophecy

Notice also the following Roman Catholic private prophecy related to the U.S.A. (**bolding** in the original):

> Our blessed Mother through Father Gobbi of the Marion Movement…provided several messages…
>
> On November 15, 1990: **Mary spoke about the great trial coming to the United States and for all humanity. The Blessed Mother specifically mentions the United States will know the hour of weakness and of poverty as well as "the hour of suffering and defeat". The thunder of God's justice will have arrived:**
>
> **…"…Sins of impurity have become ever more widespread, and immorality has spread like a sea which has submerged all things. Homosexuality, a sin of impurity which is against nature, has been justified; recourse to the means of preventing life have become commonplace, while abortions--these killings of innocent children--have spread and are performed in all areas of your homeland. The moment of divine justice and of great mercy has now arrived. You will know the hour of weakness and poverty; the hour of suffering and defeat; the purifying hour of the great chastisement…"** America will know poverty and defeat! Those are strong statements … [54]

The "hour of trial" that the Bible speaks of (Revelation 3:10) seems to begin with the Great Tribulation, "the time of Jacob's trouble" (Jeremiah 30:7) -- recall that Jacob placed his name on the progenitors of the U.S.A. and British-descended peoples (Genesis 48:3-16).

While it is true that various predictions from the Marian Movement have been shown to be false (details on a variety of claimed Marian apparitions are included in my book *Fatima Shock!*), the fact is that Joe Biden and Kamala Harris have promoted aspects of sexual immorality that the Bible warns against.

The Bible shows that sexual and other forms of immorality are destructive (Romans 1:18-32) and that what looks like the strongest military power will be destroyed in the end times (Daniel 11:39).

Debt

The U.S.A. has greatly increased its debts this century.

The Bible warns that debt, and having to borrow from foreigners, is a curse that would hit those who received various biblical blessings as they became more disobedient (Deuteronomy 28:15,43-46).

Notice the following levels of official US debt:

- January 20, 2009, $10,626,877,048,913.08, date Obama-Biden Administration inaugurated.
- January 19, 2017, $19,944,429,217,106.77, date Obama-Biden leave office, replaced the next day by Trump-Pence inaugurated.
- December 14, 2020, $27,512,762,494,452.83, date Electoral College declares Biden-Harris team to take office on January 20, 2021 to replace Trump-Pence.
- January 7, 2021, $$27,683,250,886,478.03, date Electoral College votes were "certified."

Official US debt nearly doubled under the Obama-Biden Administration. It also increased by about $8 trillion in the four years of the Trump-Pence Administration.

This is dangerous.

Yet, the Biden-Harris team intends to increase the debt much further:

> Joe Biden is assembling a team of liberal advisers who have long focused on the nation's workers and government efforts to address economic inequality. … All are outspoken supporters of more government stimulus spending to boost growth,[55]

> Joe Biden and his transition team are preparing for an early, all-out push to pass an ambitious new stimulus bill, … the passage of a broad economic aid package and, where legislation is not necessary, a series of executive actions aimed at advancing his priorities [56]

Joe Biden announced on January 8, 2021 that he and his team are working on putting a stimulus package together quickly — and that it will be costly.

> Joe Biden said Friday he is assembling a multitrillion-dollar relief package … "The price tag will be high," he said … "in the trillions of dollars." [57]

Such "relief" packages increase debt. The U.S.A. is walking a dangerous line on its debt that will not end well.

Let us also consider that there is a prophecy in Habakkuk, written about 2600 years ago, about debt which is preceded by the following:

> [2] Then the Lord answered me and said:

> Write the vision And make it plain on tablets, That he may run who reads it. (Habakkuk 2:2)

The Bible says that the 'debt prophecy' to be revealed later in Habakkuk 2 is so significant that those who read it should run—essentially that they should take steps because the results will be horrific. Joe Biden and many other American politicians have not run away from increasing U.S.A. debt—that will be to the nation's peril.

The Bible warns about something that will happen to a heavily indebted nation. Notice what the Hebrew seer Habakkuk wrote over 2,600 years ago:

> ³ For the vision is yet for an **appointed time; But at the end** it will speak, and it will not lie. Though it tarries, wait for it; Because **it will surely come**, It will not tarry ... ⁵ Indeed, because he transgresses by wine, He is a proud man ... ⁶ "Will not all these take up a proverb against him, And a taunting riddle against him, and say, 'Woe to him who increases What is not his—how long? And to him who loads himself with many pledges'? ⁷ **Will not your creditors rise up suddenly?** Will they not awaken who oppress you? **And you will become their booty.** ⁸ Because you have plundered many nations, **All the remnant of the people shall plunder you...** (Habakkuk 2:2-3,6–8).

Notice that what is to happen is so bad, that people who read the prophecy should run, when it is time for it to be fulfilled. Since that prophecy is to be fulfilled at the appointed time of the end, it is still for the future, but perhaps not too far distant in the future. No nation has ever been in as much total debt as the U.S.A.

The "U.S. is highly vulnerable to loss of confidence by foreign creditors."[58] U.S. government debt is "extremely vulnerable to foreign attack because of the high percentage of foreign ownership — almost 40% of the market."[59]

Interestingly, in the past, one foreign creditor, China, has raised concerns about the U.S. debt that are so serious, that its potential dumping of that debt has been called China's "nuclear option"[60] against the U.S.A.—an option that involves no military intervention, but that could greatly harm the U.S.A.

Others have been concerned that Russia will perhaps encourage something like this when the timing is right. European leaders have been working for years to establish a new reserve currency for the world, partially with the intent to remove the U.S. dollar from its position as the world's primary reserve currency.

Those in Iran and some of the Arab lands, along with nations such as Brazil and India have discussed plans for the removal of the dominance of the U.S.A. in global trade as well. The former President of Brazil, Lula, even claimed that eliminating the U.S. dollar's reserve currency status was one of the reasons that the BRICS alliance (Brazil, Russia, India, China, and South Africa) was formed. [61]

The Bible clearly warns against cheapening the money supply and encourages having money hold its value (Proverbs 25:4 Isaiah 1:25, Ezekiel 22:18-22). Yet policies enacted under the Obama and Trump Administrations, following certain other administrations, have ignored these warnings.

No nation in the history of humankind has ever accumulated as much debt as the United States of America (because the U.K. may have close to the highest amount of per capita debt,[62] its fate would be similar). Destruction is coming.

However, the relationship between debt accumulation and prophesied destruction remains unapparent to many.

Because there is a time lag, many ignore that there will be real consequences (cf. Ecclesiastes 8:11; Habakkuk 2:3,6-8). Yet, these increases of debt are utterly dangerous.

When the time comes that the Federal Reserve is no longer able to keep interest rates artificially low, the U.S.A. will continue past the point of no return. That will become one of the final factors that will cause creditors to rise up and destroy the U.S.A.

The Economy

While pushing biblically immoral ideas is bad for the economy, it should be noted that economies vary. A modern reality is that being the world's *de facto* reserve currency has helped prolong the U.S.A.'s dominance.

When the U.S. dollar is no longer the world's reserve currency, this will hurt the U.S.A. financially. Increasing debt, including "quantitative easing," is a form of dishonest profits that is not something that God approves of and will punish the U.S.A. for (cf. Ezekiel 22:13-16).

Inflation will eventually hit the U.S.A. extremely hard. As the world becomes less attached to the American dollar, many financial jobs and opportunities will be in places other than the U.S.A. Eventually, but not yet, the U.S.A. dollar will become worthless (worth no more than the scrap or sentimental value of the cotton-paper it is printed on).

Will it always be straight downhill for the economy of the U.S.A.?

No.

There are some reasons to have some temporary optimism. The longer there is some economic stagnation in parts of the economy that governmental COVID-19 policies contributed to, the more demand tends to build up, and an increase in demand may prolong the economy (look for the Biden-Harris Administration to take/get credit for getting COVID-19 under control). In addition, technological and other developments may temporarily support the U.S. economy — as can reductions of regulatory burdens.

Some policies of the Biden-Harris Administration may help. Others see problems. The Biden-Harris team looks to increase various regulations and impact some industries negatively (such as the fossil fuel industry). Various ones see their proposed policies and cabinet selections as a refreshing change that they hope will fuel economic growth and shared prosperity.

Notice what was told to a king who was prophesied to lose his kingdom:

> [27] Therefore, O king, let my advice be acceptable to you; break off your sins by being righteous, and your iniquities by showing mercy to the poor. Perhaps there may be a lengthening of your prosperity. (cf. Daniel 4:27)

Repentance can prolong prosperity, but promotion of sin leads to destruction. But, it is not expected that Joe Biden or Kamala Harris will push for scriptural national repentance.

The Bottom Line

Like many politicians, Joe Biden and Kamala Harris, do not meet the following leadership criteria:

> [21] Moreover you shall select from all the people able men, such as fear God, men of truth, hating covetousness; (Exodus 18:19)

44

³ The God of Israel said, The Rock of Israel spoke to me: 'He who rules over men must be just, Ruling in the fear of God. (2 Samuel 23:3)

This does not bode well for the U.S.A.

Furthermore, the Bible warns against the type of moral decline that is occurring in the U.S.A.:

¹² Therefore thus says the Holy One of Israel: **"Because you despise this word, And trust in oppression and perversity, And rely on them,** ¹³ **Therefore this iniquity shall be to you** Like a breach ready to fall, A bulge in a high wall, Whose breaking comes **suddenly, in an instant**. (Isaiah 30:12-13)

But how can this happen to the U.S.A.? It will likely happen with a combination of events. Notice:

⁵ "Moreover the multitude of your foes Shall be like fine dust, And the multitude of the terrible ones Like chaff that passes away; Yes, it shall be in an instant, suddenly. ⁶ You will be punished by the Lord of hosts with thunder and earthquake and great noise, With storm and tempest and the flame of devouring fire. (Isaiah 29:5-6)

The debt situation of the U.S.A. is putting it at risk of being unable to recover should it be hit by weather problems, terrorist acts, war, riots, solar flares, severe earthquakes, civil unrest, devastation of their genetically-modified food supplies, food shortages, and/or various pestilences–an intensity of "sorrows" such as Jesus discussed in Matthew 24:4-8 leading up to the time of the Great Tribulation. Political issues, climate change, trade policies, communication's deals, and other events are pushing the U.S.A. to a position that will encourage its takeover

45

someday. Disasters, especially if there is an ElectroMagnetic Pulse (EMP) attack, a severe solar flare storm, devastating hurricane (s) something like a massive volcanic eruption and/or massive earthquake could be part of a so-called "perfect storm" of events that could set up the U.S.A. for destruction.

Consider the devastation of New Orleans by Hurricane Katrina. Multiply that by other disasters. The U.S.A. is at risk. Notice, also, the following related to Dr. Michio Kaku's assessment of Yellowstone:

> Scientists assure us that one day the absolutely massive Yellowstone supervolcano will once again experience a Category 8 eruption, and if it happened today it would "literally tear the guts out of the United States of America" ... "Instead of having 50 states of the Union, we would have 30 states of the Union." [63]

A 'perfect storm' of disasters, internal strife, and misplaced confidences will make the U.S.A. a nation that can be defeated.

Many sorrows that the U.S.A. will face, like severe weather problems, diseases and earthquakes, will happen in the future, irrespective of who is in the White House (Amos 4:7-10; Luke 21:11). Joe Biden and Kamala Harris look to hasten the day of destruction.

3. Europeans are Not Pleased

After the Edward Snowden leaks came out during the Obama-Biden Administration, Europeans became incensed about U.S.A. espionage. So much so, that various Europeans believe this caused irreparable damage to relations with the U.S.A.

The Obama-Biden Administration greatly offended the Europeans when the Europeans found out via Snowden's release of documents that the Americans were spying on the European Union (E.U.) itself, spying on European leaders, and because they learned that the U.S.A. treated the others in the Five Eyes much better than the Europeans.

The Five Eyes is an intelligence alliance comprised of Australia, Canada, New Zealand, the United Kingdom and the United States. The continental Europeans were not part of that alliance.

Many in Europe feel that they were misled, lied to, or otherwise betrayed by the government of the U.S.A.

The documents leaked by Edward Snowden showed that the U.S.A. only listed the Anglo-Saxon nations of Canada, United Kingdom, Australia, and New Zealand as "close friends."[64] They also showed extensive amounts of spying against the European Union. In addition, some documents revealed that the U.S. spied on Germany to a similar degree as to the amount of spying it has done on China.[65]

The German publication *Der Spiegel* reported that the U.S. considered Germany to be a 'third rate partner' in at least one of the leaked documents.[66] It was reported in 2014, that the Obama-Biden Administration may have succeeded in "helping to convert it {Germany} from an ally into an adversary."[67] Germany will become an adversary according to Isaiah 10:5-11 and the Obama-Biden Administration contributed to that.

These, and other related matters, outraged the Germans and many other continental Europeans. So, also did the disparaging comments about the European Union from then Assistant Secretary of State Victoria Nuland in 2014. [68]

Despite the fact that the Europeans were insulted by Victoria Nuland in the Obama-Biden Administration, in January 2021 "it was reported Nuland … is to be nominated as undersecretary of state for political affairs, effectively the third-ranking U.S. diplomat." [69] That is something else expected to displease the Europeans.

Donald Trump Has Had an Impact

Before the 2016 election, the *Washington Times* warned:

> **A European Union army is not in America's interests**
>
> Germany, France and Italy — cling to delusions of grandeur. They have drawn up plans for a European Union army and deeper EU defense integration, claiming that this will enhance European security.
>
> An EU army, however, is not the solution to Europe's problems. It will undercut NATO, reduce U.S. influence in Europe, and strengthen the strategic position of Vladimir Putin's Russia.[70]

It is true that such an army will reduce U.S. influence and not work out in America's interests, nor is it what Europe needs.

And then came Donald Trump.

Donald Trump berated Europe, in particular, for trade issues and currency valuation. [71]

He pulled the U.S.A. out of the Paris climate accords and the Iranian nuclear deal, both of which were backed by the European Union.

He also upset many in Europe by calling NATO "obsolete." [72]

Furthermore, he called out many European countries for not paying enough on the military in relationship to NATO (North Atlantic Treaty Organization). He also threatened to NOT defend NATO nations that would not spend more on their militaries.[73]

Many in Europe were offended by Donald Trump and his comments, even prior to his election. [74] Even back in late 2015, Karl-Theodor zu Guttenberg, former German Defense Minister, called Donald Trump "that blonde lunatic named Donald."[75]

Europe Did NOT Stand Still

While many in the Trump-Pence Administration thought that the Europeans would have no choice but to cater to their demands, the Europeans moved in a way many did not expect.

In less than one year after the Trump-Pence Administration began, 25 European countries formed a pan-European military alliance called the Permanent Structured Cooperation (PESCO). [76]

While some have resisted it, there have been more and more calls for Europe to develop its own military force that will not have to defer to the U.S.A. [77]

Europe already has its own space agency, satellite system, and many other military components.

Since the Obama-Biden Administration pushed the Europeans to spend more on their militaries, do not expect that a Biden-Harris Administration will discourage European military spending.

The U.S.A. needs to be careful about what it has been asking for. Although it is true that the U.S.A. contributes a vastly disproportionate share to NATO, I have warned that the more the Europeans themselves spend, the more independent they will be about their spending and military priorities.

Since the Bible says that Europe will have a "great army" (Daniel 11:25), we know Europe will end up with a great army. It will also end up with a substantial navy (Daniel 11:40). Europe is prophesied be an amazingly marvelous military power that will surprise the world (Revelation 13:3-4).

This will not end well for the U.S.A.

Trade

But beyond that, many Europeans have been incensed because of the election of Donald Trump. And still are:

> "You will never rewind history," the E.U.'s Vice President and foreign affairs chief Josep Borrell told TIME in a Nov. 16 interview. Four years of President Donald Trump, who labeled the bloc a "foe" and has slapped tariffs on European goods, has left Europeans with a lasting sense that U.S. support is not necessarily dependable, he says. "Trump has been a kind of awakening. And I think we should stay awake," Borrell says. "We cannot say 'oh

Trump is no longer there, we can go back to our previous state of mind.'"[78]

Notice also the following:

> **Europe Won't Get Any Relief on Trade From Biden**
> ... a President Biden would do as little as possible on trade. But the world will not stand still. ... Europe would be ... challenging.[79]

Now, we would expect trade negotiations with Europe to continue and some type of agreements will happen. In the spirit of accommodation and personal interest, many of the "standards" of the European Union will be adopted by the U.S.A., as well as by nearly all of the countries of the world. The Arab nations will most likely agree with many of the standards as they seem to be destined to form a brief end-time alliance with the Europeans.

Yet, misunderstandings and differences of opinion will occur.

Trade wars and/or serious trade disputes will most likely arise.

It is likely that trade issues will be a factor in Europe ultimately turning against the U.S.A.

Europe to Reorganize

Some are concerned that the Biden-Harris Administration will be overly hostile to Russia and this ultimately will lead to war. [80]

U.S.A. positions on Russia have often differed from European positions. French President Macron even declared "Russia is a very deeply European country." [81] Since Europe is at times more trusting of Russia than the

U.S.A., anti-Russian positions from a Biden-Harris Administration may also push Russia to later assist the Europeans when they decide to completely turn against the U.S.A.

Germans and others see the U.S.A. declining. Europe will go in a direction that U.S.A. leaders, including its 'foreign policy experts,' do not comprehend (Daniel 11:39; Isaiah 10:5-11).

Notice something that was claimed by the German Press:

> **For 100 years, the United States was the leader of the free world. ... It is time for Europe ... to step into the void. ...** Europe's turn.[82]

Europe wants to rise up. And also militarily:

> Germany's respected Frankfurter Allgemeine Zeitung newspaper, meanwhile, even contemplated the "unthinkable" in an editorial: a German bomb. [83]

While European leaders have begun to publicly challenge reliance on the U.S.A., biblically, the time will once again come when Europe cannot be trusted militarily (Isaiah 10:5-11; Daniel 11:21-39; Lamentations 1:2).

The U.S.A., itself, has repeatedly shown the Europeans that it does not trust them, yet it sometimes will trust them too much. According to the Bible, the time will come when the U.S.A. will find that continental Europe will be an enemy (cf. Isaiah 10:5-11) and not an ally (Ezekiel 23:4,9-10): "All her friends have dealt treacherously with her; They have become her enemies" (Lamentations 1:2).

As I stated on the radio back in 2016, I believe that Europe will cooperate with the U.S.A. as long as it feels the relationship is beneficial, and then (as prophecy foretells) turn against the U.S.A.

The Bible is clear that there will be problems in Europe (Daniel 11:41-43), yet it also shows that Europe will undergo several reorganizations (Revelation chapters 16-18), and the two reorganizations in Revelation 17:12-13 specifically will not turn out well for the U.S.A. (cf. Daniel 11:39) or the Arab world (cf. Daniel 11:40-43).

GPS and Galileo

The U.S.A. has military issues that many do not realize.

Back in 2009, despite denials from the U.S. Air Force,[84] I warned that the U.S.A. was likely to have problems with its Global Positioning System (GPS) and may need to rely on Europe's future Galileo system for some of its military needs.[85]

My warnings were based upon my biblical understandings (e.g. Isaiah 10:5-11; Daniel 11:39; Revelation 13:4; 2 Peter 3:8-12) as well as my previous military experience. I knew full well that military spokespersons did not always tell the full truth.

In late 2009, Air Force General Kevin Chilton publicly confirmed that the U.S.A. did NOT have enough satellites for military purposes.[86]

At the same time, Europe's Galileo satellite system was in process. In March 2002, the European Directorate-General Energy and Transport produced an 'information note' which stated:

> Galileo will underpin the common European defence policy that the Member States have decided to establish. **There is no question here of coming into**

conflict with the United States which is and will remain our ally, but simply a question of putting an end to a situation of dependence. If the EU finds it necessary to undertake a security mission that the US does not consider to be in its interest, it will be impotent unless it has the satellite navigation technology that is now indispensable. Although designed primarily for civilian applications, Galileo will also give the EU a military capability. [87]

Some in Europe have long wanted to be independent of the U.S.A.

It should also be understood that there were "early objections from the Americans who thought a rival system to GPS might be used to attack its armed forces."[88] Former U.S. Deputy Secretary of Defense, Paul Wolfowitz also wrote to a European leader raising objections to it back in 2001.[89]

Yet the later Obama-Biden Administration did not object, but instead encouraged the Europeans to develop it. [90]

Then in late July 2010, it was announced that the U.S.A. would rely on Europe's Galileo system for part of its own military defense.[91] This is biblically very dangerous (cf. Lamentations 1:1-2; Daniel 11:39).

Could Europeans have the ability to know where people are? Well, since most cellphones now have 'GPS,' those with them in the U.S.A. also face the very real possibility that Europeans will be able to track where they are as well as to control other aspects of cellphones. Yet, relatively few in the U.S.A. realize this.

By the time all of Galileo is fully implemented it may be too late for the U.S.A. to get enough of its own satellites up to change this.

Because of the Snowden leaks, the Obama-Biden Administration pledged to share U.S.A. data collection espionage techniques with the Europeans,[92] and it would not seem that a Biden-Harris Administration will stop all of that.

Having the U.S.A. dependent upon Europe's Galileo system for part of its military defense communications is dangerous. Galileo appears to give the rising European power a unique offensive and defensive capability against the U.S.A. (cf. Daniel 11:39; Revelation 13:3-4).

It is dangerous to have a potential enemy control portions of one's military communications systems. But the U.S.A. has done that.

Many in the U.S.A. do not seem to realize that once Europeans are spending more for their militaries, that they will also expect to have more independence from the U.S.A. as to how military might will be used.

Because they do not put much stock in biblical prophecies, Joe Biden and Kamala Harris are not expected to truly understand the threat that Europe poses and are expected to enable its rise.

4. Islam and Prophecy

Donald Trump upset many when he implemented a travel ban on people from various Islamic-dominated nations. He said he did so to reduce potential terrorist threats.

Joe Biden's plan is to quickly change that policy:

> On the first day of his presidency, president-elect Joe Biden intends to rescind Donald Trump's travel bans on travellers from 13 countries, most either majority-Muslim or African nations. [93]

That travel ban specifically included Syrians.

Is there any possible threat from Islamic and/or Syrian refugees?

Yes, there are prophecies that say so. Consider the following two:

> [25] ... There shall be terror within (Deuteronomy 32:25)

> [8] The Lord sent a word against Jacob, And it has fallen on Israel. [9] All the people will know -- Ephraim and the inhabitant of Samaria -- ... [11] Therefore the Lord shall set up The adversaries of Rezin against him, And spur his enemies on, [12] The Syrians before and the Philistines behind; And they shall devour Israel with an open mouth. (Isaiah 9:8-9, 11-12)

The U.S.A. will have more terrorist attacks.

Syrian refugees are a potential problem.

The Bible clearly is prophesying problems from Syrians and Palestinians. And this would be expected to include terrorism.

While Donald Trump slowed down the flow of Islamic migrants to the U.S.A., there are already many here. More would be expected to come under the Biden-Harris Administration, as Joe Biden himself has called for. And while most such immigrants are not a threat, biblically some are.

And yes, terror is prophesied to hit the U.S.A. And this is also consistent with prophecies in Psalm 83 of a group that seems to include most, if not all, of the Trump Administration banned peoples being part of it. Joe Biden wants them in.

Notice something from Psalm 83:

> 3 They have taken crafty counsel against Your people, and consulted together against Your sheltered ones.
>
> 4 They have said, "Come, and let us cut them off from being a nation, That the name of Israel may be remembered no more."
>
> 5 For they have consulted together with one consent; They form a confederacy against You: 6 The tents of Edom and the Ishmaelites; Moab and the Hagrites; 7 Gebal, Ammon, and Amalek; Philistia with the inhabitants of Tyre; 8 Assyria also has joined with them; They have helped the children of Lot. (Psalms 83:3-8)

The above peoples are in lands dominated by Islam in North Africa and the Middle East.

Psalm 83 is very likely to involve terrorism.

Why?

Because taking "crafty counsel" sounds like plotting terrorism. Notice also that a deal will happen involving Assyria, which is prophesied to take over the U.S.A. and U.K. per Isaiah 10.

The King of the South

The Obama-Biden Administration wanted a coalition of Arab nations in the Middle East and North Africa to help deal with terrorism and other matters.[94] It is expected that a Biden-Harris Administration would support a coalition of nations in that region and believe that will contribute to peace.

While peace is good and cooperation can be a good thing, there are Islamic writings, as well as biblical ones, that show that an Islamic coalition will not always turn out well.

Notice the following from the *New Encyclopedia of Islam*:

> The last days, as described in Islam, are marked by the figures of Gog and Magog (Juj wa Jajuj), the Mahdi, the Antichrist (Dajjal), and Jesus ... Gog and Magog, representing the forces of chaos, have been kept at bay ... At the end of time, chaos will break through the wall of Divinely imposed order, and the world will succumb to "outer darkness". At the same time, it is believed, there will be a countercurrent, or a brief return to the state of spiritual lucidity and primordial integrity that obtained at the dawn of time. This is the reign of the Mahdi, the "rightly guided one"...
>
> The reign of the Mahdi will be followed by that of the Antichrist ... once the Antichrist has led away his

followers, Jesus will then come to destroy the Antichrist in the closing moments of the cosmic drama.

Belief in the Mahdi has been rejected by noted Sunni authorities ...[95]

The Bible tells of a leader called the King of the South (Daniel 11:40-43) that sounds similar to the Mahdi that various ones in Islam are looking forward to. Even without this Mahdi, 2016 saw the world's largest military exercise (called North Thunder) composed of 20, basically Sunni-Muslim, nations,[96] which are consistent with the peoples prophesied to get together later (Daniel 11:40-43). World events are aligning with properly understood biblical prophecy.

Some in Islam seem to believe that the reign of the European Beast (Revelation 13:1-10) and Antichrist (Revelation 13:11-17; 1 John 4:1-3) will happen after the Mahdi's death.

Now, biblically, this is true, to a degree, for the Arab lands. However, the Bible shows that the Beast of Revelation (also called the King of the North in Daniel 11) and the final Antichrist (a European-supporting false religious leader) will rule in Europe and over some of the American lands (Daniel 11:39), prior to the European reign over Arab lands (Daniel 11:40-43). Hence, the Bible teaches that the final Antichrist will have power prior to the death of the biblical King of the South.

Although the belief in a "Mahdi" apparently had been a minority Sunni view and has had rejection by some Sunni authorities, "the Muslim World League issued a *fatwa* in October of 1976 commanding Sunni Muslims to believe in the concept of an Islamic Savior called the Mahdi."[97]

It should also be noted that some Sunni groups, like the Muslim Brotherhood want a Caliph to arise and rule an Islamic caliphate that includes all the territory from northwest Africa through the Middle East and even further east.[98]

However, Sunnis (who vastly outnumber the Shi'ites) should not change their anti-Mahdi views (various Sunni scholars also agree[99]) or want a Caliph, because of what the Bible shows will happen. Shi'ites also would do well to recognize that just because someone may claim to be the final Imam (or Mahdi), does not mean that God will agree that he should be followed. Neither Sunnis nor Shi'ites should support one who will appear to possibly be the final Imam/Caliph in the next decade or so (the two that have recently claimed to be are not). A major leader of Islamic lands will apparently make such claims and rise up, but will be defeated soundly (Daniel 11:40-43; Ezekiel 30:2-8).

Expect the Biden-Harris Administration to take steps that will help lead to the rise of the King of the South.

Iran and Prophecy

Joe Biden wants to have the U.S.A. rejoin the nuclear deal with Iran that Donald Trump pulled the U.S.A. out of. [100]

He also might be more willing than the Obama-Biden Administration had been to trigger enforcement provisions if he feels Iran has violated portions of the agreement.

After Donald Trump's election, Iran declared it would pursue development of nuclear powered ships.[101]

Because Bible prophecy indicates that it will be primarily Arabic nations that support the final King of the South (Daniel 11:40-43; Ezekiel 30:1-8), though with some (probably temporary per Daniel 11:25-26) support from

Turkey and possibly Pakistan and/or Afghanistan, it is not biblically possible that Iran can truly be the leader of the Islamic world as it seems to want to be. Also, because it is basically due east of Jerusalem, Iran should not be considered to be a candidate to be the final 'King of the South' of biblical prophecy.

Despite its posturing and relative military strength, Iran will be somehow effectively neutralized (cf. Ezekiel 32:24). This could perhaps be from an attack involving Israel and/or internal civil unrest -- this could also include electromagnetic (EMP) or similar weapons used against Iran (Jeremiah 49:34-39).

It is of prophetic interest to note that the small nation of Israel is prophesied to one day be attacked by some that seem to have connection to Iran and its ally Syria (Isaiah 22:1-14).

In January 2021, it was reported, "Iranian lawmakers have submitted a bill seeking the government by law to commit to Israel's destruction by the year 2040, Iranian state media ISNA reported." [102]

Iran may decide to strike out against Israel, and likely Jerusalem (cf. Isaiah 22:7-8) if it determines that it should. If it is frustrated with the Biden-Harris Administration policies or delays, that may very well be a factor in it taking prophesied military action.

Iran has weapons that can cause damage. Furthermore, the U.S.A. itself, as well as the State of Israel, are vulnerable to EMP type attacks and even items such as biological weapons, chemical weapons, terrorism, nuclear weapons, dirty bombs, etc. because of a conflict involving Iran, Syria, and/or others.

But should this attack occur, this would NOT be the final destruction of the U.S.A. Prophetically, Iran would not end up faring well (cf. Ezekiel 32:24-25).

Jesus and the Koran

Many people do not realize that most Muslims, whether they are Shia or Sunni, expect Jesus (who they tend to call the *son of* Mary/Miraim/Marium) to return at the time of judgment. Notice what the Koran (Qur'an) teaches:

> *043.057*
> **YUSUFALI:** When (Jesus) the son of Mary is held up as an example, behold, thy people raise a clamour thereat (in ridicule)!
>
> **PICKTHAL:** And when the son of Mary is quoted as an example, behold! the folk laugh out,
>
> **SHAKIR:** And when a description of the son of Marium is given, lo! your people raise a clamor thereat
>
> *043.061*
> **YUSUFALI:** And (Jesus) shall be a Sign (for the coming of) the Hour (of Judgment): therefore have no doubt about the (Hour), but follow ye Me: this is a Straight Way.[103]

My hope and prayer related to the above is that when Muslims do see Jesus return, they hopefully will accept the truth of His coming after He explains who He is.

Islam and the Bible Look for a Peace Deal

In Islam, there are writings that there will be a seven-year peace deal with a Roman Catholic European leader that will be broken:

Rasaullah [Muhammed] said: "There will be four peace agreements between you and the Romans [Christians]. The fourth agreement will be mediated through a person who will be the progeny of Hadrat Haroon [Honorable Aaron -- Moses' brother] and will be upheld for seven years.[104]

General anarchy and bloodshed, that no Arab household will be spared from it Then a life of peace as a result of a peace agreement between you and the Banil Asfaar (Romans) which they will break and attack you with a force consisting of eighty flags and under each flag will be an army of twelve thousand men.[105]

Those writings appear to be consistent with the following biblical prophecy:

[26] And the people of the prince who is to come Shall destroy the city and the sanctuary. The end of it shall be with a flood, And till the end of the war desolations are determined. [27] Then he shall confirm a covenant with many for one week; But in the middle of the week He shall bring an end to sacrifice and offering. And on the wing of abominations shall be one who makes desolate, Even until the consummation, which is determined, Is poured out on the desolate. (Daniel 9:26-27)

The above is referring to a deal or covenant that has a time element attached to it. The 'one week' time element has generally been understood anciently to mean a seven-year deal (e.g. Hippolytus of Rome [106]), that will be broken in the middle of it (after 3 1/2 years, which is a half a week also per Irenaeus of Lyon [107]). The 'with many' would seem to indicate that 'many' nations, as opposed to one or two, are agreeing to something.

The reference to a "prince" is referring to the leader of the developing European empire. One way to show this is to realize that it was the people of the Roman Empire of the 1st century that fulfilled the portion of Daniel 9:26 as they destroyed the city (Jerusalem) in 70 A.D. Because of other biblical passages (Daniel 8:25; 11:23-24) this is generally considered to be a "peace deal" by prophecy watchers.

So, both biblical and Islamic prophecy tell of a time when there is a peace deal between the Europeans and others that will one day be broken.

The confirmation of a seven-year portion of some 'peace' agreement by the relatively powerless "prince" is an event that will set off what could be considered the final clock of many prophesied end-time events. Including the last 3 ½ years of the U.S.A. Since various Protestant and other prophecy watchers are also looking for this deal, it is likely it will not look obvious to most when it is confirmed. But, make no mistake about it, this will be an important prophetic event. Even though many looking for it will not believe it, even when it is told to them (cf. Habakkuk 1:5).

In the future, a Biden/Harris Administration may attempt to get Israel to accept the type of "peace deal" that Daniel 9:27 seems to refer to. This looks to be something to occur in the first term of the Biden/Harris Administration.

A confirmation of a particular deal with a time element in it by a European 'prince' will set the countdown for the rise of the Beast and the destructive Great Tribulation.

5. Could Joe Biden or Kamala Harris be the Antichrist?

Antichrist is a term that strikes fear in many.

Related to Joe Biden, Roman Catholic Archbishop Carlo Maria Viganò, a former papal ambassador to the United States, declared in an interview:

> "It would be an irreparable disaster if Joe Biden, who is heavily suspected of being complicit with the Chinese dictatorship, would be designated as president of the United States," ...

> "I think of his intention to condemn us all to wear masks, as he has candidly admitted. I think of the fact that, incontestably, he is only a puppet in the hands of the elite, who are ready to remove him as soon they decide to replace him with Kamala Harris ... Joe Biden, who is subservient to the globalist ideology and its perverse, anti-human, antichristic, infernal agenda." [108]

By referring to Joe Biden as "antichristic," this shows he is believed by the Archbishop to be at least promoting the totalitarian Antichrist agenda. A Biden-Harris Administration may also be expected to support parts of what has been called a "reset" by the World Economic Forum.

Notice also the following related to Kamala Harris:

> Conservative Texas pastor Robert Henderson said politicians like Vice President-elect Kamala Harris are driven by the "Antichrist spirit,".[109]

While some feel that way about them, could the actual and

final Antichrist be Joe Biden or Kamala Harris?

No.

The Four Verses

The terms 'antichrist' and 'antichrists' are only used in the Bible five times. They are only found in four verses of the Bible—all written by the Apostle John.

Those verses are 2 John 7, 1 John 2:18, 1 John 2:22, and 1 John 4:3.

Let's examine the four verses in the Bible that specifically mention "antichrist," starting with 2 John 7:

> 7 For many deceivers have gone out into the world who do not confess Jesus Christ as coming in the flesh. This is a deceiver and an antichrist (2 John 7).

This scripture says that antichrists are deceivers "who do not confess Jesus Christ as coming in the flesh." Does this verse allude to a leader that is simply not acknowledging that there was a person named Jesus?

This seems highly unlikely, as even most atheists acknowledge there was one referred to as Jesus Christ who lived in the flesh. This doctrine of Antichrist might have something to do with not completely believing a member of the Godhead actually emptied Himself of His divinity to become human (even though that is what happened according to Philippians 2:6–7) and/or not humbling oneself to truly accept Christ to live His life in their flesh. The former belief is a doctrine that certain faiths officially adopted because of the Council of Constantinople in 381 A.D.

John also wrote the following related to Antichrist:

¹Beloved, do not believe every spirit, but test the spirits, whether they are of God; because many **false prophets** have gone out into the world. ² By this you know the Spirit of God: Every spirit that confesses that Jesus Christ has come in the flesh is of God, and every spirit that does not confess that Jesus Christ has come in the flesh is not of God. ³ And this is the spirit of the **Antichrist**, which you have heard was coming, and is now already in the world (1 John 4:1–3).

This scripture similarly states that the "spirit of Antichrist" is not confessing that Jesus Christ has come in the flesh. It also shows that some of Antichrist's teachings began when John was still alive.

These verses specifically tie in the idea that false prophets have the spirit of Antichrist. Thus, it would seem consistent with these passages to conclude that the final Antichrist would or could be a *false prophet* (which is a term that John uses later in the Book of Revelation 16:3).

In addition, John also wrote:

> ¹⁸ Little children, it is the last hour; and as you have heard that the Antichrist is coming, even now many antichrists have come, by which we know that it is the last hour. ¹⁹ They went out from us, but they were not of us; for if they had been of us, they would have continued with us; but they went out that they might be made manifest, that none of them were of us. ²⁰ But you have an anointing from the Holy One, and you know all things. ²¹ I have not written to you because you do not know the truth, but because you know it, and that no lie is of the truth. ²² Who is a liar but he who denies that Jesus is the Christ? He is antichrist who denies the Father and the Son (1 John 2:18–22).

These scriptures show that while there will be a final Antichrist, even since John's time, there have been pretended and false believers. These passages also state that if people were true believers, they would have continued with John's practices.

Thus, because the faithful true Christians have continued with the practices of the Apostle John (like Passover,[110] Luke 22:8-23), there is reason to believe that at the end, the final Antichrist will endorse some type of religion that is somehow against those faithful Christians who hold to some of John's known practices.

Since all the verses mentioning 'antichrist, discuss some aspect of theology, they show that the final Antichrist is mainly a religious figure. So, that rules out Joe Biden or Kamala Harris.

Who is the Antichrist?

If neither Joe Biden nor Kamala Harris can be the final Antichrist, who is the final Antichrist?

Well, before answering that, there is another to eliminate.

Although many Roman Catholics and Protestants believe that the first Beast of Revelation 13, also known as 666, is the Antichrist, he is not. While he will oppose God (cf. 2 Thessalonians 2:3-4), the Beast of Revelation 13:1-10 is not mainly a religious leader.

The second beast in Revelation 13:11-17, however, is primarily a religious leader (even though he also has political power as one of his "two-horns" represents):

> [11] Then I saw another beast coming up out of the earth, and he had two horns like a lamb and spoke like a dragon. (Revelation 13:11)

Jesus is the "lamb of God," yet this false Antichrist leader looks, to the deceived, like a lamb. He promotes religious worship and is also referred to in other scriptures as "the false prophet" (Revelation 16:13; 19:20; 20:10). He is likely to be considered a current or future saint by his followers.

It is he who is the final 'Antichrist,' as all the specific warnings mentioning "antichrist" in the Bible are discussing religious leaders.

Furthermore, despite some views that the final Antichrist is Muslim as they try to tie 'Mystery Babylon the Great' in with ancient Babylon, that is wrong. Babylon in the Book of Revelation is a city on seven hills (Revelation 17:5-9). Revelation is referring to a city such as Rome, even according to Roman Catholic scholars and not ancient Babylon,[111] as the ancient city of Babylon was on a flat plain.

Chinese, Roman Catholic, and Eastern Orthodox Prophecy

There is a Chinese prophecy dating back to the Middle Ages that appears to somewhat warn against the Antichrist, while another may indicate he and others he associates with are from Europe:

> Beautiful people come from the West.[112]

> All negative forces are subservient...China now has a saint. Even if he is not that great a hero.[113]

It is likely that these 'prophecies' were written down after part of China had been exposed to the Bible. Europe is west of China and was considered to be part of the far west when the above prophecy was written. The Antichrist may seem beautiful to some as he will be able to perform miracles and will claim peace. The final Antichrist would likely be considered a 'saint' by many and is expected to come from an area west of China. He most certainly would not be a true hero.

The final Antichrist would also appear to be the one warned about as the antipope in various Roman and Orthodox Catholic writings. Also, notice the following:

> *Priest Herman Kramer* (20th century): This false prophet possibly ... usurps the papal supremacy ... His assumed spiritual authority and supremacy over the Church would make him resemble the Bishop of Rome ... He would be Pontifex Maximus, a title of pagan emperors, having spiritual and temporal authority. Assuming authority without having it makes him the False Prophet ... **Though he poses as a lamb, his doctrines betray him ...** His principles and dogmas to be accepted **... it will comprise emperor-worship** ... with the persecution of true believers.[114]

> *Priest A. Maas* (20th century): Nearly all commentators find Antichrist mentioned in the Apocalypse ... many scholars identify Antichrist with the beast which had "two horns, like a lamb" and spoke "as a dragon" ... the Abbot really believes that Antichrist will overthrow the Pope and usurp his See ...[115]

> *Helen Tzima Otto* (2000): The anti-pope – Episcopal of the Beast, alias the false prophet ...[116]

Note: I also agree with Priest Kramer that the false prophet will promote emperor worship as that is consistent with what Revelation 13:11-17 teaches.

Also, notice that the commentators of the *Rheims New Testament* seem to agree with my assessment about an antipope:

Antichrist, if he ever were of or in the Church, shall be an Apostate and a renegade out of the Church, and he shall usurp upon it by tyranny, and by challenging worship, religion, and government thereof, so that himself shall be adored in all the Churches of the world which he list to leave standing for his honor. And this is to sit in the temple or against the Temple of God, as some interpret. If any Pope did ever this, or shall do, then let the Adversaries call him Antichrist.[117]

Thus, from biblical and even certain Roman Catholic perspectives, it appears that the false prophet, final Antichrist, may be a demon-influenced "pope" (cf. Revelation 16:13; 17:18).

The final Antichrist is likely to be one who changes, though he does not clearly seem to be changing, the Roman Catholic religion. It seems that this is the individual who has been warned against in both biblical and private Catholic prophecies.

Neither Joe Biden nor Kamala Harris Can Be the Final Antichrist

As stated before, because they are primarily political figures, neither Joe Biden nor Kamala Harris can be the final Antichrist.

However, they do hold anti-Christian positions on matters such as sexual morality, right to life, and debt accumulation.

The Biden-Harris Administration is expected to contribute to the rise of the final Antichrist, as well as the final European Beast power.

6. The End of the United States Before Two Presidential Terms?

Is there any prophetic reason to believe that the destruction and end of the U.S.A. can come before the completion of the next two presidential terms? Could the end of the U.S.A. happen before 2029?

Yes.

There is an old tradition that the prophet Elijah taught that there would be six thousand years for humans to rule under Satan's kingdom, followed by one thousand years of abundance in the kingdom of God.

That Jewish view is consistent with the views of early Christians and some associated with them. Some believed that since God made/recreated the world in six days and rested on the seventh day (Genesis 2:1-3), that humans would have 6,000 years to live on the earth under Satan's influence. Humans surviving the Great Tribulation and Day of the Lord will have a 1,000 year period to be under Christ's reign (the original creation of the universe may have been billions of years earlier c.f. Genesis 1:2; Isaiah 45:18); The 6,000 plus 1,000 years equals God's seven thousand year plan.

Here are specific traditions related to this from the Jewish Babylonian Talmud:

> R. Kattina said: Six thousand years shall the world exist, and one [thousand, the seventh], it shall be desolate, as it is written, And the Lord alone shall be exalted in that day {Isaiah 2:11}.

> Abaye said: it will be desolate two [thousand], as it is said, After two days will he revive us: in the third

day, he will raise us up, and we shall live in his sight {Hosea 6:2}.

It has been taught in accordance with R. Kattina: Just as the seventh year is one year of release in seven {Leviticus 25:1-7}, so is the world: one thousand years out of seven shall be fallow, as it is written, And the Lord alone shall be exalted in that day' {Isaiah 2:17}, and it is further said, A Psalm and song for the Sabbath day {Psalm 92:1}, meaning the day that is altogether Sabbath — and it is also said, For a thousand years in thy sight are but as yesterday when it is past {Psalm 90:4}.

The Tanna debe Eliyyahu teaches: The world is to exist six thousand years. In the first two thousand there was desolation; two thousand years the Torah flourished; and the next two thousand years is the Messianic era … [118]

And while there are some errors from a Christian perspective in the above, Jewish sages have taught that there is a six thousand year plan, that the current two thousand years essentially represents the Messianic/Church era (which looks to end by 2031), and that a one thousand year period remains.

Note: I inserted the scriptures quoted or alluded to above within {} as many are in the footnotes associated with the above.

In a Jewish Midrash (a term that means "exposition" or "investigation"), Pirke De-Rabbi Eliezer comments:

Six eons for going in and coming out, for war and peace. The seventh eon is entirely Shabbat and rest for life everlasting: [119]

Again, that is consistent with the view that the world as we know it will end after 6,000 years, followed by a 1,000 year millennium.

Matthew Henry's Commentary on the Whole Bible (a Protestant source), related to Leviticus 25:1-7, states:

> In the seventh year shall be a sabbath of rest unto the land, v. 4. Jews collect that vulgar tradition that after the world has stood six thousand years (a thousand years being to God as one day) it shall cease, and the eternal sabbath shall succeed ...

Elsewhere, the Bible itself teaches that a thousand years seems to be as one day to God. This is a concept from both the Old and New Testaments:

> 4 For a thousand years in Your sight Are like yesterday when it is past ... 12 So teach us to number our days, That we may gain a heart of wisdom. (Psalm 90:4, 12)

> 8 But, beloved, do not forget this one thing, that with the Lord one day is as a thousand years, and a thousand years as one day (2 Peter 3:8).

Is it not interesting that after stating a thousand years is as a day, the Psalmist was inspired to write that our own days are limited and we should number our days that we may have the heart of wisdom? Understanding approximately where we are in the 6,000 years, thus, looks to be a wise thing to do.

Notice also the following from the Book of Genesis (the first book of the Bible) which supports the view of a day being like a thousand years:

¹⁶ And the Lord God commanded the man, saying, "Of every tree of the garden you may freely eat; ¹⁷ but of the tree of the knowledge of good and evil you shall not eat, for **in the day** that you eat of it you shall surely die." (Genesis 2:16-17)

How long was Adam's day before he died?

⁵ So all the days that Adam lived were nine hundred and thirty years; and he died. (Genesis 5:5)

So, Adam died "in the day"--a day that was not too much less than 1,000 years long.

A day is to God as 1,000 years and that looks to be part of His plan.

Now, some may say, don't the Jews say that we are in year 5781 which runs from September 19, 2020 to September 7, 2021?

Yes, the claimed year is 5781 AM (anno mundi) by the Jews.

However, the Jewish year claim confuses many people as the numbers do not add up with scripture.

Many Jewish scholars have recognized this error throughout history, and believe it was intentional. [120] The numbers related to the years were changed in the early 2nd century C.E./A.D. and are now off approximately 210 years.

When the proper biblical chronologies are used, both Christians and Jews should realize that the 6,000 years likely will not extend more than a decade from now.

Last Days Fit When 1,000 Year Days are Understood

Based upon certain calculations that I am currently aware of, it seems that Adam and Eve were created and/or apparently left the garden of Eden between roughly 3959-3972 B.C. It is most likely that the 6,000 years began once Adam sinned as Adam had not rebelled before then.

This would mean that when Jesus began to preach (roughly 27 A.D., about four thousand years later) He started preaching late in thousand-year day four and then into day five. Day four is the middle of seven prophetic thousand year days, hence the fourth day is not one of the "last days."

Interestingly, in the German language, the fourth day of the week is Mittwoch which means mid-full or mid-week — what we call in English Wednesday is not one of the last days, but the middle day.

Anyway, it is logical that days five, six, and seven would have been considered as part of the "last days" by the early disciples.

That being so, this helps explain why some New Testament figures indicated that they were in the last days:

> 14 But Peter, standing up with the eleven, raised his voice and said to them, "Men of Judea and all who dwell in Jerusalem, let this be known to you, and heed my words. 15 For these are not drunk, as you suppose, since it is only the third hour of the day. 16 But this is what was spoken by the prophet Joel: 17 *'And it shall come to pass **in the last days**, says God, That I will pour out of My Spirit on all flesh* (Acts 2:14-17).

¹ God, who at various times and in various ways spoke in time past to the fathers by the prophets, ² has **in these last days spoken to us by His Son**, whom He has appointed heir of all things (Hebrews 1:1-2).

If there is no 6,000 year plan of human rule followed by a 1,000 year millennial reign, then the New Testament statement above, about then being in the *last days,* makes little sense. But, since God does have a 7,000 year plan, these statements do make sense. And that also explains why the end has not come yet--there is still a little more time in "the last days."

Since Jesus was preaching into "the last days," He must have been doing some of that in day five of the seven one thousand year days.

Furthermore, since the events in Acts 2 appear to have happened c. 31 A.D. (or 30 A.D.), this would suggest that the 6,000 years should be up by 2031--if not earlier.

Jesus was, of course, alive before 31 A.D., and perhaps the last days began as early as 28 to 30 A.D.

The Bible teaches that "the testimony of Jesus is the spirit of prophecy" (Revelation 19:10).

God's word teaches that prophecy is important (cf. Isaiah 46:9-11).

In the early second century, Church of God leader Papias of Hierapolis (who was a hearer of the Apostle John and a friend of Polycarp of Smyrna) taught:

> … there will be a period of a thousand years after the resurrection of the dead, and that the kingdom of

Christ will be set up in material form on this very earth ... [121]

The idea of a six/seven thousand year plan was taught by early Greco-Roman Catholic saints as well. In the late second century, Irenaeus of Lyon taught:

> ... that apostasy which has taken place during six thousand years. For in as many days as this world was made, in so many thousand years shall it be concluded. And for this reason the Scripture says: "Thus the heaven and the earth were finished, and all their adornment. And God brought to a conclusion upon the sixth day the works that He had made; and God rested upon the seventh day from all His works." This is an account of the things formerly created, as also it is a prophecy of what is to come. For the day of the Lord is as a thousand years; and in six days created things were completed: it is evident, therefore, that they will come to an end at the sixth thousand year... [122]

> But when this Antichrist shall have devastated all things in this world, he will reign for three years and six months, and sit in the temple at Jerusalem; and then the Lord will come from heaven in the clouds, in the glory of the Father, sending this man and those who follow him into the lake of fire; but bringing in for the righteous the times of the kingdom, that is, the rest, the hallowed seventh day; and restoring to Abraham the promised inheritance, in which kingdom the Lord declared, [123]

So, Irenaeus claimed that the seven days of creation were a type of the seven thousand year plan, that the end of humanity's rule would end after the 6,000 years ended, and would be followed by a type of rest in the Lord's kingdom.

Hippolytus was, and is still considered to have been, an important Roman Catholic leader and saint:

> Hippolytus was the most important theologian and the most prolific religious writer of the Roman Church in the pre-Constantinian era … [124]

Notice something Hippolytus wrote in the early 3rd century:

> And 6,000 years must needs be accomplished, in order that the Sabbath may come, the rest, the holy day "on which God rested from all His works." For the Sabbath is the type and emblem of the future kingdom of the saints, when they "shall reign with Christ," when He comes from heaven, as John says in his Apocalypse: for "a day with the Lord is as a thousand years. "Since, then, in six days God made all things, it follows that 6,000 years must be fulfilled. [125]

Notice therefore that "**the most important theologian and the most prolific religious writer of the Roman Church in the pre-Constantinian era**" taught the 7,000 year plan (6,000 for humankind, followed by 1,000 from God). According to him and others, the 6,000 years end when Jesus returns.

And presuming that the great tribulation begins (Matthew 24:21-22) 3 ½ years before the end of the 6,000 years (the latest date which appears to be 2031), then the 6,000 years would be up no later than 2028. Since that is before January 19, 2029, which is the end of the second presidential term from now, presuming this 'last days' calculation is correct, this is why the end of the U.S.A. could occur by then.

It also needs to be understood that there are two types of *last days* referred to in the New Testament. When some were stating that they were in the last days, this indicates the latter days of the 7,000 year week. However, in other places, New Testament writers sometimes are referring to the time of the final generation before Jesus returns as being the last days, as they indicate that this was not for the same time as they were writing (cf. 2 Peter 3:3).

The destruction of the U.S.A. is coming soon. Expect that the Biden-Harris Administration will, therefore, take actions that will lead to it.

Getting back to Hippolytus, since he understood the "week" in Daniel 9:26-27 to be a seven-year period, his calculation would point to the deal of Daniel 9:27 occurring 7 years prior to the end of the 6,000 years. If so, that would have that deal confirmed in the timeframe of the first Biden/Harris Administration.

In the early 20th century, the late Sabbatarian leader G.G. Rupert taught the 6,000 year plan followed by a 1,000 year millennium. [126]

The idea of 6,000-7,000 year plan is not unique to those who are Sabbath-keepers. According to even Roman Catholics, parts of this view have long been the belief of those who claim to believe at least part of the Bible:

> *E. Culligan* (20th century): ... the time of the First Resurrection will end ... It is the time when the Seventh Millennium will set in, and will be the day of Sabbath in the plan of creation ... It has been the common opinion among Jews, Gentiles, and Latin and Greek Christians, that the present evil world will last no more than 6,000 years ... Christians and Jews, from the beginning of Christianity, and before, have taught that 6,000 years after the creation of Adam and Eve, the consummation will occur. The

period after the consummation is to be the seventh day of creation--the Sabbath ... St. Jerome said, "It is a common belief that the world will last 6,000 years." ... I believe that as the last days come to an end so will the sixth day of creation. [127]

Priest G. Rossi (19th century): One day with the Lord, then, is as a thousand years, and a thousand years as one day. It is the common interpretation that each of the six days of creation is equivalent to one thousand years for the future existence of human generations. Now God employed six days in the creation of this world; this world, then, shall last only six thousand years; the Sabbath, or seventh day, representing eternity.

The learned Cornelius A. Lapide, in his erudite commentaries on the Bible, in the second chapter of Genesis and twentieth chapter of the Apocalypse, attests that it is a common opinion among Jews and Gentiles, among Latin and Greek Christians, that this world shall last only six thousand years.

Christian writers have taught the same opinion from the beginning of Christianity ... we learn, then, that the six mystic days of creation are intended to signify the six thousand years of the world's duration. The seventh day, which, to the exclusion of the other six days, God has in a special manner blessed and sanctified, must be taken for the happy eternity of the blessed saints, for the holy sabbath of everlasting rest, for the blissful duration of perpetual peace, and perfect happiness to the elect of God, who will behold him face to face, praise, love, adore, and glorify him forevermore. ...

For those who desire to examine many more Fathers and doctors of the Church, we will here supply a pretty long list of them: St. Cyprian, Lib. IV. Epist. 5; St. Ambrose, Comment. 2 Thess. 11; the famous book of St. Hypolitus, De Antichristo; St. Hilary, Can. in 17 Matt.; St. Augustine, De Civit Dei, Lib. XX. chap. 17; Lactautius Firmia- nus, Lib. VII. chaps. 14 and 15; St. Anastatius Sinaita, Lib. XVII. inHexamcr; St. Justin ad ortodox, Quest. 71; St. Germanus, Patriarch of Constantinople, St. Cyril; the ancient writer, Q. Julius Hilarion; Cassiodorus, St. Isidore, Victorinus, Rabanus, Bellarmine, Genebrardus, etc., and many others, who, to use the words of Q. Julius Ililarion, unanimously affirm: Summa complela annorum sex millium fiet resurrectio. At the end of six thousand years shall take plaw the yeneral resurrection. Our kind critics will please pay some attention to these numerous and grave authorities before they disapprove what we here state.

From all the above-mentioned authorities we learn, then, that the six mystic days of creation are intended to signify the six thousand years of the world's duration. The seventh day, which, to the exclusion of the other six days, God has in a special manner blessed and sanctified, must be taken for the happy eternity of the blessed saints, for the holy sabbath of everlasting rest, for the blissful duration of perpetual peace, and perfect happiness to the elect of God, who will behold him face to face, praise, love, adore, and glorify him forevermore. Amen!

Assuming now as pretty certain that this world shall last only about six thousand years, because such is the common opinion and expectation of humanity, how many years more, it may be asked, still remain to the end of this world. [128]

While some Roman Catholics may point out that their church does not currently teach that, the truth is that early leaders it considers to be saints, did. Furthermore, the book by Emmett Culligan (also known as "the Culligan man") "was blessed by Pope Paul VI, 1966," and the book by priest Rossi was approved by his theological superior for publication.

That being said, time is getting short.

Hindu Writings?

Now, you might be a Hindu or otherwise skeptical of biblical prophecies. As it turns out, certain interpretations of Hindu prophecies point to basically the same time (though they use a 5,000 year period, which started about 1,000 years later). Notice the following:

> Lord Krishna says that Kali Yuga will end 5,000 years after its beginning, giving way to a Golden Age. …

> Hindus believe that human civilization degenerates spiritually during the Kali Yuga, which is referred to as the Dark Age because in it people are as far removed as possible from God. …

> The timeline also indicates that the ascending Kali Yuga, which is the current epoch in which we are living, will end in 2025 CE. [129]

Now, from a biblical perspective this is a bit too early for the new utopian age (Christians would refer to that age as the millennial kingdom of God). Yet, other Hindu writings point to this leader being a warring one. Here are two such reports:

Kalki, who is considered the last Avtar or incarnation of Vishnu or the Supreme Being, who will establish the Age of Truth or Age of Purity on Earth.... As agreed by all the religious prophecies, the Awaited One will not be a man of peace like Jesus Christ or Buddha, but a man of war who will destroy evil and establish righteousness on the earth. [130]

Bhagwan Kalki would be a spiritual master of the highest order with the deadly combination of a wise dictator (Chanakya of the modern era) ... [131]

So, essentially, a warring leader that Hindus will accept (for a time) is to possibly rise up in 2025. Since the Bible shows that "All who dwell on the earth will worship" (Revelation 13:8) the warring Beast power (Revelation 13:1-4), and since this Beast leader's reign is 42 months (Revelation 13:5), if he were to rise up in 2025, 42 months later would be sometime in 2028 or 2029.

While this author relies on biblical prophecies, those Hindu reports are eerily consistent with Jesus returning between 2028-2031. It may well be some of the Kalki prophecies have demonic-connections intended to encourage those of the Hindu faith to (temporarily) accept the coming European Beast power.

Now it has been said that "if" is the biggest two-letter word in the English language.

So, to summarize this chapter:

1. If as the School of Elijah taught, that God inspired Elijah to state that the world as we have known it would last 6,000 years, to be followed by a thousand year sabbatical time, which Jewish tradition (Talmud, Tractate Sanhedrin [97a]) and early

Christian traditions records (e.g. Irenaeus, a hearer of Polycarp. Adversus haereses, Book V, Chapter 30:4), then we are getting close to the end of that time.

2. And if, consistent with scriptures in both the Old and New Testaments, we can apply the concept that a thousand years is as a day to God (Psalm 90:4; 2 Peter 3:8).

3. And if, as generally understood in the Church of God that Jesus was killed and resurrected no later than the Spring of 31 A.D. on Passover.

4. And if we can presume that the "last days" of a 7,000 year prophetic week began AFTER the middle day (day 4), then the last days prior to the "sabbatical" time, which some would refer to as the millennial Kingdom of God would last two thousand years.

5. And if when Peter referred to being in the last days (Acts 2:17-18) and since Hebrews 1:1-12 teaches that "God ... has **in these last days** spoken to us by His Son."

6. Then adding 2,000 years to a period of time leads to the end of the 6,000 years no later than 2031 (and it could be earlier than that).

7. Since the Great Tribulation is expected to start 3 1/2 years prior to that (cf. Revelation 12:14; 13:5) subtracting 3 1/2 years from the Spring of 2031 would be late in 2027.

8. Understand that the U.S.A. is prophesied to be taken over near the rise of the Beast and start of the Great Tribulation (cf. Daniel 11:39; Jeremiah 30:7; Matthew 24:21-22).

9. Therefore, since the end of two full U.S.A. presidential terms would end in January of 2029, these prophetic understandings point to the end of the U.S.A. prior to two full presidential terms.

10. This is also consistent with certain Hindu and Roman Catholic prophetic writings as well.

It looks like from certain Jewish, biblical, Christian, Roman Catholic, and Hindu perspectives (and yes others associated with those faiths have other opinions), that the end of the U.S.A. will happen before the next two four-year presidential terms end.

7. 19 Reasons Why Joe Biden and Kamala Harris are Apocalyptic

The last book of the Bible is referred to as "Revelation" or the Apocalypse (the Greek term which means revealing, and this was given to the Apostle John on the island of Patmos, per Revelation 1:9). For purposes of this section, we will use the term "apocalyptic" to mean related to events that lead to the end-time events prophesied in the Bible.

There are reasons to believe that the rising of the prophesied final ten-horned beast power (Revelation 13:1) and possibly the destruction of the United States could take place under a Biden-Harris Administration if it lasts two full terms (eight years, perhaps 12 if it becomes a Harris Administration and certain events do not unfold in a particularly understood timeline). And this destruction is likely to include terrorism and partial nuclear devastation.

Catholic Cardinal Stafford (while head of the *Apostolic Penitentiary of the Holy See* [132]) claimed that Barack Obama and Joe Biden were "aggressive, disruptive, and apocalyptic." Notice what he reported in November 2008 about the then coming Obama-Biden Administration:

> Barack Obama... asserted, *"We are not only going to win this election but also we are going to transform this nation.........The first thing I will do as President is to sign The Freedom of Choice Act........I put Roe at the center of my lesson plan on reproductive freedom when I taught Constitutional Law...........On this issue I will not yield.."*... The content and rhetoric of Obama and Biden have elements similar to those described earlier: aggressive, disruptive and apocalyptic ... My use of the word "apocalyptic" would be

emphatically biblical, rooted in the understanding of the Book of the Apocalypse.[133]

Furthermore, because Joe Biden and Kamala Harris do not seem to understand many end-time biblical events, this perhaps will lead each of them to be more accommodating to the rise of the King of the North and King of the South powers than one who believes and understands end-time prophecy would likely support.

Here are nineteen specific reasons indicating some of how Joe Biden and/or Kamala Harris are "apocalyptic":

1. The timing of their administration. We are in the last days of God's 6,000/7,000 year plan. A day to God is like 1,000 years (2 Peter 3:8; Psalm 90:4), and since it is wise to know the days (Psalm 90:12), this is a reason that both would seem to be apocalyptic. We are getting close to the end of the time God gave humans to rule themselves. Thus, we are close to the start of the Great Tribulation and the fulfillment of related prophecies in the Book of Revelation. There are prophetic reasons to conclude that the U.S.A. cannot last for two-full presidential terms.
2. The Obama-Biden Administration seemed supportive of the type of confederation that will lead to the formation of the final King of the South of biblical prophecy (Daniel 11:40-43). A Biden-Harris Administration is expected to do the same, if not more.
3. The Biden-Harris team is interested in increasing debt, which the Bible condemns as a curse (Deuteronomy 28:15,44). They intend stimulus and other projects that are expected to increase the debt of the U.S.A. Increasing national debt will lead to destruction at the appointed time of the end (Habakkuk 2:3–8). They will

88

not be able to reverse enough of the debt to stop Habakkuk 2:3-8 from being fulfilled.

4. The Obama-Biden Administration often encouraged increased military spending by the Europeans. And while American taxpayers may see this as a good thing, this increased spending will help lead to the rise of the prophesied King of the North, who is to be the final leader of the Beast of Revelation (Revelation 13:1-10). The Biden-Harris Administration is expected to promote European military spending which would help enable the rise of the King of the North/Beast power who will be in league with the final Antichrist.

5. Donald Trump's rise has also spurred the Europeans to further unify among themselves, especially when combined with the Brexit vote that Donald Trump encouraged. While the Bible shows the Europeans will have difficulties being together (Daniel 2:41-43), it also shows that they will reorganize and unite (Revelation 17:12-13). Donald Trump has been pointed to by various European leaders as 'proof' that Europe needs more unification and distance from the U.S.A. A Biden-Harris Administration will not stop European distancing — though it may sometimes temporarily appear to do so.

6. Joe Biden and Kamala Harris both claim to be Christians, yet support restrictions on religious speech and actions, while specifically pushing for a sexual agenda that the Bible says ends in death and destruction (cf. Romans 1:18-32; Jude 7).

7. Joe Biden does not seem to realize the inherent danger for the U.S.A. to rely on Europe's upcoming Galileo "GPS" for part of the U.S.A.'s military defense. This would appear to give the rising European power a unique offensive and defensive capability against the U.S.A. (cf. Daniel 11:39; Revelation 13:3-4). It is dangerous to have a potential enemy control portions of one's military communications systems.

8. Humans should eat what is good (cf. Isaiah 55:2). Joe Biden, like others before him, has made statements supporting the use of genetically-modified organisms (GMOs) to be consumed as foods.[134] Increased reliance on GMOs by the United States puts the nation at major risk for nearly complete crop failures. The Bible warns that famines (Matthew 24:7) and food shortages (Revelation 6:5-6) are coming and the Biden-Harris Administration may further help set the stage for this.

9. The Biden-Harris Administration wants to increase Islamic immigration into the U.S.A. The Bible prophesies "There shall be terror within" (Deuteronomy 32:25). The Bible also specifically warns of problems from Arabic peoples in the end times (Psalm 83:3-8). Some Syrians, including some already in the U.S.A., may take terroristic actions as that too is consistent with biblical prophecy (cf. Isaiah 9:8-9, 11-12).

10. By focusing too much on threats from China and almost always considering the Europeans as some type of allies, a Biden-Harris Administration is currently not expected to reverse the Asian 'pivot' strategy of the Obama-Biden Administration. Unless that changes, this pivot will help result in destruction of the U.S.A.

11. The incoming Biden-Harris Administration has made some statements suggesting they are not fully in agreement with the right of free speech. A "famine" of the word is prophesied (Amos 8:11) and it is possible that they could authorize steps that could lead to that.

12. Kamala Harris is an admitted adulterer and Joe Biden has been accused of inappropriate behavior by enough women that suggests this charge is credible (as have some comments he has made about it). By encouraging and not discouraging aspects of biblical immorality, they are setting the U.S.A. up for punishment (Isaiah 30:12-13; Romans 1:18-32) that has

and will include troubles, violence, weather problems, earthquakes, food shortages, and pestilences (Mark 13:7-8; Luke 21:10-11). The time will come when, these problems will further worsen.

13. Joe Biden and Kamala Harris believe their policies will lead to more peace. We will one day hear proclamations of false peace and safety and the Bible warns repeatedly that end-time destruction will follow those declarations (1 Thessalonians 5:3; Jeremiah 6:14-15).

14. Jesus warned about a coming time of pestilences as part of the beginning of sorrows (Matthew 24:4-8). Actions and/or inactions by Joe Biden and/or Kamala Harris will likely put the U.S.A. at increased risk of problems from pestilences.

15. Joe Biden's and Kamala Harris' misstatements show that they are not always honest. This is not good (Proverbs 29:2; Psalm 15:1-4). Some statements by him and Kamala Harris are consistent with those warned about for the last days in 2 Timothy 3:1-6.

16. Religious views by Joe Biden and Kamala Harris show that they are somewhat 'ecumenical.' An ecumenical power is warned about in the Bible and is expected to rise up in the end times (Zechariah 2:6-8; Revelation 17; 18). I expect them to make inter-faith/ecumenical supporting statements.

17. Joe Biden has made statements supporting losses of privacy, increased surveillance, and favoring unlimited government control. This type of thing will be exploited by 666 of Revelation 13:16-18.

18. Joe Biden and Kamala Harris seem to be the type of people who would support the 'peace deal' of Daniel 9:27, which precedes the start of the Great Tribulation by a few years.

19. Divisive statements from Joe Biden and Kamala Harris are expected to result in division and protests. Jesus taught, "Every kingdom divided against itself is

brought to desolation, and a house divided against a house falls" (Luke 11:17b).

Because the deal of Daniel 9:27 has not yet been made, let alone confirmed, the Great Tribulation, itself, cannot begin until at least 2025. It thus, however, may possibly begin in a year that Joe Biden or Kamala Harris could be president.

Joe Biden, Kamala Harris, and all others, should open their Bibles and practice genuine Christianity, before they are subject to being misled by the modified, ecumenical religion that will come upon the whole world (cf. Revelation 13:3-4).

The Bible itself does NOT teach true Christian unity until *after* the return of Jesus Christ (Zechariah 2:10-12), but instead warns against the "Babylonian" movement that will precede it (Zechariah 2:6-9).

Of course, it is not only the United States that needs repentance as God "now commands all men everywhere to repent" (Acts 17:30). But a nation that has been blessed by God should lead the way (cf. Deuteronomy 4:5-6; Luke 12:48).

Notice some other destructive prophecies that could affect the U.S.A. and some of its allies:

> [22] Yes, a fire has blazed from my anger, it will burn right down to the depths of Sheol; it will devour the earth and all its produce, it will set fire to the footings of the mountains. [23] I shall hurl disasters on them, on them I shall use up all my arrows. (Deuteronomy 32:22, NJB)

> [33] I will scatter you among the nations and draw out a sword after you; your land shall be desolate and your cities waste. (Leviticus 26:33)

Because of biblical prophecy, the fact that the Bible teaches that to "everyone to whom much is given, from him much will be required" (Luke 12:48), and its hypocrisy (Isaiah 10:5-6, KJV), the U.S.A. is expected to be amongst the first to suffer from the Great Tribulation (Matthew 24:21).

This period is also called the "time of Jacob's trouble" (Jeremiah 30:7). Although some may object because they believe that the U.S.A. and its Anglo-Saxon allies are more "righteous" than those that will destroy it, this too is prophesied (Habakkuk 1:13; 2:5-8; Isaiah 10:5-19).

The last President of the United States, whoever that may be, will further set the stage for the beginning of the Great Tribulation.

When the Great Tribulation starts, it will not be a good time for the U.S.A., or for its Anglo-Saxon allies (nor the nation of Israel). Biblical ("sudden destruction" 1 Thessalonians 5:3; Deuteronomy 29:23-28), Hopi,[135] and Kenyan[136] prophecies suggest possible nuclear devastation and/or other high-tech destruction of at least some of their lands.

Notice some of what Jesus Himself taught:

> [21] For then there will be great tribulation, such as has not been since the beginning of the world until this time, no, nor ever shall be [22] **And unless those days were shortened, no flesh would be saved**; but for the elect's sake those days will be shortened (Matthew 24:21-22).

> [36] Watch therefore, and pray always that you may be counted worthy to escape all these things that will come to pass, and to stand before the Son of Man. (Luke 21:36)

Jesus taught people to watch what was happening in the world and pray to be able to escape the coming tribulation (in Acts 2:38 the Apostle Peter specifically taught people to repent and be baptized, as well).

The Great Tribulation itself is further described in Revelation 6:9–11 (the fifth seal that seems to occur because the faithful church has suffered martyrdom), Lamentations, Daniel, and other parts of the Bible. The Great Tribulation will include the destruction of the United States.

Brief Sequential Summary of Selected End-Time Events

As far as certain end-time events go, here is a brief semi-sequential summary of some items:

1. The basic sequence is that certain sorrows, violence, and troubles will continue (Mark 13:7-8). This is happening.
2. The 'peace' deal of Daniel 9:27 is confirmed. Deals have been proposed, but the biblical one has not yet been made nor confirmed. Because of prophecies related to the destruction of Damascus (Isaiah 17:1) and great damage to be done to Jerusalem (Isaiah 22:8-9), one or both of those events may well precede the deal of Daniel 9:27.
3. A King of the North (who was a 'prince' in Daniel 9:27) and a King of the South (Daniel 11:27) will arise. They will make a lying deal together (Daniel 11:27). Europe will get a "great army," while "a very great and mighty army" will form in the Middle East and North Africa (Daniel 11:25, 40-43). We are seeing the foundations for this now with calls for European and Islamic unity and militaries.
4. Animal sacrifices will begin (cf. Daniel 9:27). (Note: It is possible that the King of the South could arise up prior to Daniel 9:27 or even after the sacrifices resume

as could the King of the North). Some Jews would like to start them now, but the Israeli government will not currently allow it.

5. The gospel then will have been preached enough to the world as a witness for the end to come (Matthew 24:14). This seems to be related to the 'short work' of Romans 9:28. As far as God is concerned, Matthew 24:14 has not be sufficiently fulfilled yet.

6. Europe will reorganize into ten 'kingdoms' (not necessarily nations as some have improperly insisted upon) and give power to the Beast per Revelation 17:12-13.

7. The abomination of desolation will then be set up (Matthew 24:15; Mark 13:14) because of actions of the King of the North and Jewish sacrifices will be stopped (Daniel 9:27, 11:31, 12:11). The most faithful expect to continue to tell what is happening until they are somehow stopped (cf. Amos 8:11-12).

8. A decree is to be issued (Zephaniah 2:1-3), perhaps by one of the two witnesses. Then the most faithful Philadelphians will 'fly' to the wilderness (Revelation 12:14-16) and those in Judea will flee (Matthew 24:15-19; Mark 13:15-18). Prior to when the Great Tribulation starts, the two witnesses will support the work and near its start, they will get special power to do their job (Revelation 11:3).

9. Bolstered by the Antichrist/False Prophet, then the Great Tribulation will begin (Matthew 24:21-22; Mark 13:19-20; Daniel 11:39, 12:1b; cf. Habakkuk 2:7-8) and the U.S.A. attacked. This will eliminate the indebted U.S.A. and its Anglo-Saxon descended allies as nations (Daniel 11:39; Jeremiah 30:7; Habakkuk 2:7-8).

10. The King of the South will shortly later push against the King of the North and get eliminated (Daniel 11:40-43).

11. About 28-29 months after the Great Tribulation began, the sixth seal will be opened, there will be a

'blood moon' and a darkened sun (Revelation 6:12; Joel 2:30-31), then the 144,000 of Revelation 7:1-8 will be sealed.

12. Shortly thereafter, the seventh seal will be opened (Revelation 8:1-6) and year-long Day of the Lord (Isaiah 34:8) will begin with trumpet blasts, plagues, etc. (Revelation 8-7-13; 9:1-21; 11:13-14).

13. The crashing of Wormwood into the earth will occur after the third trumpet blast (Revelation 8:10-11). Some might call this Planet X hitting the earth.

14. The gathering for Armageddon will begin related to the sixth trumpet blast (Revelation 8:13-19; 16:12-16).

15. Then at the seventh trumpet (Revelation 11:15) Jesus will return to establish the millennial kingdom of God.

The Great Tribulation should be about 3 1/2 years after the peace deal (Daniel 9:27) is confirmed, and right after the King of the North tries to proclaim peace and safety (1 Thessalonians 5:3) to throw people off (cf. Daniel 11:24) for his invasion plans.

The U.S.A. will need to be further weakened in several ways for this to occur. Rising immorality will weaken the U.S.A., as will debt, and relying on international agreements. These are, sadly, in progress.

The Europeans will need to be stronger militarily, as well as use deceit, to begin their attack. They are working on a variety of military projects.

While everything certainly will not be a Biden-Harris Administration's fault, they are, inadvertently, leading the U.S.A. towards the apocalypse.

8. Native American Prophecies

There are legends related to certain native American prophecies that seem to foretell of the time when the white-people of the Americas will be destroyed somehow and that their tribes would again rise:

Native Prophets of the Americas

Until recent years it has been a controversial step for native leaders to publish their prophecies, but many are now coming forward because the prophecies themselves contain a directive to go out and warn the world when certain signs appear. Signs such as the 'rain of fire' and 'gourd of ashes' (atomic warfare) and the 'shaking of the earth' (earthquakes) are seen as indications that it is time.

There are parallel themes in many of the prophecies:

1) We are entering a time of purification and can expect to witness chaos and destruction in all the kingdoms of nature.

2) It is a time for the reuniting of the races. Barriers of religion and nationality will begin to fall as all people realize their essential unity.

3) We must heal the damage done to Mother Earth, the source of life, and recognize that all living things are endowed with spirit.

4) In the coming times we will see the return of one or more Great Teachers who will guide us into the future. ...

Black Elk and Crazy Horse

Black Elk and Crazy Horse were leaders of the Lakota Sioux in the late 1800s when the US was decimating its native populations. Each had a vision of the future.

Black Elk saw that his people, after long years of destitution and death, would lose heart and the sacred hoop of his nation would be broken. But after seven generations he saw a vision of the nation being reunited and becoming part of the greater hoop of all the nations of the earth. At that time a great Prophet from the east would bring a message of hope to all people.

Crazy Horse's vision also foretold the darkness that would descend on his people. ...

The Hopi's — Waiting for Pahana

In 1948, Thomas Banyacya accepted the task of warning the world of the events foretold in the Hopi prophecies. The Hopi's, he says, had been instructed to seek a "house of mica" (glass) that would stand on the eastern shore of Turtle Island (the US). The Hopi's saw the UN building in New York as the house of mica. Beginning in 1949, they sought entry to its assembly to: 1) look for their True White Brother, 2) seek justice for Indian brothers and sisters and good people everywhere, and 3) warn leaders of the coming purification. In 1992 and again in 1993 they were able to deliver their prophecies.

Hopi legend speaks of the Pahana, or the True White Brother, who once lived with the people and would return in the time of Koyaanisquatsi, when the world was beset by fearful troubles and chaos. Then He would unite the broken tribes and reestablish balance and harmony. ...

David Gehue, Canadian Mi'kmaq, says we are in the final stages of transition when "The Great Spirit takes the earth in both hands and shakes it violently." He speaks of a mysterious person in olden times who "came from the rising sun and went to the setting sun." He warned them of the coming of seven evil cycles when the great white monster "would disperse the people to lives of misery and destitution." The mysterious brother said he would come back from the rising sun with a new spirit and power that would destroy the white monster. At that time the wisdom of the Elders would again be heeded and life restored to balance.[137]

There are *some* biblical consistencies with the above. Jesus talked about a time of transition, called "the beginning of sorrows" (Matthew 24:4-8) that we now seem to be in, that comes before the "great tribulation" (Matthew 24:21). The timing of Biden-Harris Administration fits in within the beginning of sorrows—and if it (or part of it) lasts two full presidential terms, it may well last until the start of Great Tribulation and the destruction of the U.S.A.

Furthermore, the Bible teaches that the great False Prophet will arise from Europe, which those such as Black Elk could consider as part of the east. The Bible teaches that many will accept him and his message (cf. Revelation 13:8).

The Bible warns about the type of ecumenical unity that is coming (Revelation 13:4,8;17;18; Zechariah 2:6-7), and some of the Native American prophecies seem to be encouraging this.

The Bible does teach the Anglo-Saxon descendants of Jacob will be attacked and made slaves (cf. Ezekiel 5:12; Revelation 18:13). The Native American statements related by "Native cultural specialist" David Gehue sound consistent with that.

Here is another Hopi prophecy:

The True White Brother will bring with him two great, intelligent and powerful helpers, one of whom will have a sign of a swastika (a masculine symbol of purity), and the sign of the sun. The second great helper will have the sign of a celtic cross with red lines (representing female life blood) between the arms of the cross.

When the Great Purification is near, these helpers will shake the earth first for a short time in preparation. After they shake the earth two times more, they will be joined by the True White Brother, who will become one with them and bring the Purification Day to the world. All three will help the "younger brother" (the Hopi and other pure-hearted people) to make a better world. In the prophecies, the two helpers are designated by the Hopi word for "population," as if they were large groups of people.[138]

Note the use of the swastika/cross by two of the parties, one of which is female. Then they will cooperate with the third. The first and the third may be the False Prophet and the King of the North, and the female could possibly be interpreted to be an apostate church (cf. Revelation 17).

Certain Roman Catholic prophecies seem to warn about a type of cross to be used by the Antichrist. [139] So, there may be some alignment with parts of Native American prophecies.

9. Nostradamus and the End?

Michel de Nostredame ("Michael of Our Lady," usually Latinized to Nostradamus), was a French apothecary and reputed Roman Catholic seer who published collections of prophecies that have since become famous worldwide.

Nostradamus: Original portrait by his son Cesar

One Roman Catholic writer wrote this about him:

> Nostradamus ... A member of the third order of St. Francis, he enjoyed the friendship of Pope Pius IV. He was a devout Catholic all his life ... Nostradamus was an authentic seer.[140]

Nostradamus probably is best known for his book, *Les Propheties* (The Prophecies), which was first distributed in 1555. It contained a series of 100 sets (called Centuries) of four verse-long prophetic passages (called Quatrains) that many believe were often written cryptically to help preserve his life from government/church authorities. Others believe that they were written cryptically to make

101

them subject to almost any interpretation, thus of no real predictive value.

If demons provided him with some of his information, they may have had some understandings that have resulted in some of his predictions seemingly coming to pass.

Whether Nostradamus' predictions do or do not have real predictive value, the fact is that a lot of people around the world believe that they may. Thus, some might be influenced by them. For purposes of this book, there are a couple of them that we should look at.

The first is Century 4 Quatrain 50 from Nostradamus, with the *Comment* below it from a Catholic writer:

> Under the sign of Libra, America shall reign, Shall hold power in the sky and on land, Shall never perish under Asian forces, Until seven Pontificates have passed.[141]
>
> *Comment on the above from Catholic writer Yves Dupont*: "As a great world power, the U.S.A. began its "reign" during the first World War—but it was not the *greatest* world power...In 1945, however, the U.S.A. was, by and large, the greatest world power. I think it is from the reign of Pius XII that the seven Pontificates must be counted, and this brings us to the last Pope according to St. Malachy's list—when the world will end."[142]

It appears that the above writings suggest that the end of the U.S.A. will thus be in the 21st century. And as far as Asian forces go, this could be interpreted to include terrorists from places like the Near East and other parts of Asia or maybe China. The U.S. has had troops battling "Asian forces" for some time. Potentially, if this prophecy is related to the U.S.A., its *possible* fulfillment would be relatively soon as Pope Francis is not young and is the pope after pope 111 on the Malachy list (112 pontiffs were on the list)—however since Benedict XVI is still alive, then some may think Pope Francis would not count as one of the prophesied pontiffs.

Some believe that Nostradamus' references to "Libra" means someone born under the astrological sign of Libra. Libra is supposedly from September 23 – October 22, which would therefore include Kamala Harris. Under that situation it could be implied that the end will come under Kamala Harris' leadership. And, it would not come from Asian forces, but by a European led one.

Here is a comment about that Quatrain by a writer in India (R. Chopra) in the early 21st century, who then cites Quatrain 74:

> The "seven" are the seven millennia in Nostradamus' calculations which end in A.D. 2000, which also links this quatrain to the quatrain below:

> The year the great seventh number is accomplished Appearing at the time of the games of slaughter, Not far from the age of the great millennium (2000) When the dead will come out of their graves.[143]

Now the above suggests that the forces of Asia will not be destroyed until the "seven hold the hierarchy in succession," which apparently is in the 21st century. The Bible itself does warn that the "kings of the east/sunrise" will come together at Armageddon (Revelation 16:12–16) and that a 200,000,000 man army will be destroyed (Revelation 9:13–20; 16:16). If you are Asian, you might want to warn your people now to help prevent some of them from supporting that army.

Now, if Y. Dupont is correct about the seven that "hold the hierarchy" being popes until the last one on the Malachy prophecy list, then it could suggest that Joe Biden and Kamala Harris would be among the last leaders of the America to govern before the end. And if the Asian Indian writer is correct that the seven times refers to the end coming in this millennium, the end is coming soon.

Of course, Pope Francis is becoming elderly and we cannot safely rely on non-biblical prophecy.

Yet, *if* there is soon to come an antipope who is the final Antichrist, then the following one of Nostradamus' other Quatrains (Century 10 Quatrain 66) may possibly apply to a Joe Biden or another U.S.A. presidency (perhaps the one identified as "Reb" below):

> The chief of London through the realm of America, The Isle of Scotland will be tried by frost: King and "Reb" will face an Antichrist so false, That he will place them in the conflict all together.[144]

Quatrain 66 suggests that the leader of the United Kingdom (chief of London and involving Scotland) will be influenced by the western realm of America, with the leader called "Reb" (America rebelled against England in 1776) and will encounter an Antichrist that will ultimately place them into conflict. Hence Quatrain 66 could be an end-time reference that might take place soon.

Anyway, there are some quatrains from Nostradamus that *might* point to the Biden-Harris Administration (or another U.S.A. Administration) and something terribly important happening in the 21st century. I prefer to simply state that the Bible supports the idea that the U.S.A. would have a top leader, will be destroyed by a European led power, and that major changes will happen, including its destruction, in the 21st century.

Perhaps it should be mentioned that some have interpreted Nostradamus to be predicting World War III in 2021. [145] For reasons pointed out elsewhere in this book, WWIII absolutely will not happen before 2025.

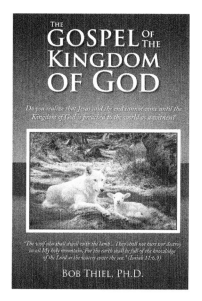

10. The King of the North, Biden-Harris, and the End of the United States and its Anglo-Saxon Allies

Joe Biden has made statements that will help lead to the rise of a European Empire as well as an Islamic confederation. These are to be led by leaders that the Bible refers to as the King of the North and the King of the South respectively.

This chapter will look into some details as to what the 11th chapter of the Book of Daniel teaches about the coming of the final King of the North as well as Roman and Orthodox Catholic prophesies associated with one called the "Great Monarch."

Some of these prophecies indicate that the "Great Monarch/King of the North" will get a "great army" (Daniel 11:25; that might increase after the U.S.A. is attacked), lead a force that will destroy the United States (Daniel 11:39), and will apparently be assisted by the King of the South (Psalm 83:3-8; Daniel 11:27). Although later, the Kings of the North and South will turn on each other, with the King of the South losing (Daniel 11:40) these outcomes are not only consistent with certain Roman and Orthodox Catholic prophecies, but some Islamic ones as well.

Some Private Prophecies of the Great Monarch

The following Greco-Roman Catholic private prophecies show that in the latter days some expect a future emperor of Europe, who with a major pope (possibly an antipope), will control the earth:

Capuchin Friar (18th century): A scion of the Carlovingian race {a descendant of Charlemagne}, by all considered extinct, will come to Rome to behold and admire the piety and clemency of this Pontiff, who will crown him, and declare him to be the legitimate Emperor of the Romans, and from the Chair of St. Peter, the Pope will lift the standard, the crucifix, and will give it to the new emperor.[146]

Venerable Bartholomew Holzhauser (died 1658): There will rise a valiant monarch anointed by God. He will be Catholic...He will rule supreme in temporal matters. The pope will rule supreme in spiritual matters at the same time. The reign of the Great Ruler may be compared with that of Caesar Augustus who became Emperor after his victory over his enemies, thereby giving peace to the world, also with the reign of Emperor Constantine the Great, who was sent by God, after severe persecutions, to deliver both the Church and State. By his victories on water and land he brought the Roman empire under subjection, which he then ruled in peace ... **The Great Monarch will** have the special help of God and **be unconquerable** …'Golden crown' refers to his Holy Roman (German) Empire …[147]

St. Ephraem (5th century): Then the Lord from his glorious heaven shall set up his peace. And the kingdom of the Romans shall rise in place of this latter people, and establish dominion upon the earth, even to its ends, and there shall be no one who will resist it.

Comment on the above from Catholic writer Desmond Birch: He is talking about some future "Kingdom of the Romans" of a "latter people." [148]

107

Desmond Birch (1996): At some point, the Great King chases an invading Moslem army back to the Holy Land ... The Great King will be crowned Holy Roman Emperor by the reigning Pope.[149]

Thus, some writers and mystics were foretelling of the rise of a future European emperor. Perhaps it should be added that on May 6, 2016, Pope Francis said he dreamed of a humane European utopia that his church would assist in bringing about.[150]

History shows that European emperors who attempt to establish dominion upon the earth tend to do that through conquering.

Is the "King of the North" European?

While the Great Monarch of Greco-Roman prophecy is European, is the King of the North of biblical prophecy also European?

The simple answer is yes.

The King of the North is discussed in Daniel 11. Now before he is called a "king," this same leader is called a prince in Daniel 9:26.

Daniel 9:27 shows that this leader takes the same actions that the King of the North does in Daniel 11:31. This prince is foretold to come from the people who destroyed the temple sanctuary in Jerusalem. Since those that destroyed the second temple in Jerusalem in 70 A.D. were part of the Roman Empire, and that prince later is to come from those people, this shows that he is European.

The Bible is also clear that the "Great Sea," where the Beasts of Daniel 7 come from, is the Mediterranean Sea (cf.

108

Numbers 34:6-7; Joshua 1:4; 9:1; 23:4; Ezekiel 47:13-16). The King of the North Beast power is not a nation like Russia, which does not border the Mediterranean Sea, but Europe which does.

Additionally, other descriptions of the Beast in the books of Daniel and Revelation show that this is a European leader.

While many do not believe that the Europeans would be willing to destroy the U.S.A., the Bible shows that despite misgivings such as "he means not so, nor does his heart think so" (Isaiah 10:7), the European power will do so anyway (Isaiah 10:5-11), and with Arabic/Turkish cooperation (Psalm 83:3-8).

While many have noticed that the European Union is not getting along that well even amongst its own member nations, the Bible specifically warns that the final European Beast power will be composed of parts that do not hold well together:

> [41] The feet you saw, part earthenware, part iron, are a kingdom which will be split in two, but which will retain something of the strength of iron, just as you saw the iron and the clay of the earthenware mixed together. [42] The feet were part iron, part potter's clay: the kingdom will be partly strong and partly brittle. [43] And just as you saw the iron and the clay of the earthenware mixed together, so the two will be mixed together in human seed; but they will not hold together any more than iron will blend with clay. (Daniel 2:41-43).

Because of Islamic terrorism, years back Geert Wilders wrote an article titled *Political Revolution Is Brewing in Europe*.[151] Islamic migrants, economic concerns, and U.S.A.-

relations will be factors in political change coming to Europe.

One of the "unintended consequences" of Donald Trump becoming president in 2017 was that the Europeans developed a pan-European military organization called Permanent Structured Cooperation, generally referred to as PESCO. By December of 2017 it had 25 European nations as part of it. [152] While PESCO is not yet capable of eliminating the U.S.A., it is helping lay the groundwork.

The Bible shows that Europe will go through at least one or two reorganizations until it gets to the point of fully supporting the King of the North/Beast power per Revelation 17:12-13. And later, it will change to betray the Church of Rome (Revelation 17:9,15-18).

Hence, Roman Catholics (and all others) would do well not to wish to follow the one known as the Great Monarch. Some, of course, do realize this as the following shows:

> The tradition of the Great King and the Holy Pope ... first emerged from the Tiburtine Sibyl, a work that may date back to AD 380-400 ...
>
> Catholic writer Paul Thigpen warns, "Looking for the Great Monarch, then, who does not appear in Scripture, might lead to overlooking the Antichrist who does. It might even lead to--a more disturbing thought--to mistaking the Antichrist for the Great Monarch. After all, lesser antichrists of the past such as Hitler and Stalin have seduced followers with visions of grand and glorious earthly kingdoms. Surely Antichrist of the last days will do the same. [153]
>
> "Could looking for the Great Monarch, then, lead believers to overlook the Antichrist, or even to

mistake the one for the other?"[154]

The reality is that many will see the King of the North as some type of 'Great Monarch' and support this Beast that the Bible warns against.

Daniel 11:23-24 warns that a similar sounding leader will gain power with a small number of supporters and devise plans against a strong power ("the strongholds").

Daniel 11:27–39

Chapter 11 of the Book of Daniel discusses various leaders, including those known as the King of the North and the King of the South. The one who will be the King of the North is prophesied to rise up "When the transgressors have reached their fullness" (Daniel 8:23), which suggests that this is about when God has had enough of the increasing immorality in nations like the U.S.A.

We will now look at a verse by verse discussion of the sequence from Daniel 11:27–39.

Why there?

Because this book is focused on the end, and verse 27 is the first place in that chapter that the "appointed time" of "the end" is mentioned (even though some verses prior also do apply).

The "appointed time" and the "end" (in Hebrew transliterated as *mowed' qets*) are terms used elsewhere by Daniel (e.g. Daniel 8:19) to describe end-time events.

In Daniel 11, there is an "appointed time" (*mowed'* Strong's #4150) in vss. 27, 29, and 35 (which indicates the events being discussed are still all in the future) (this term is also

111

used for the same time period in Habakkuk 2:3 and Zephaniah 3:18).

The specific word translated as "the end" is the same word (*qets* Strong's 7093) in vss. 27, 40, and 45 (the same Hebrew word, for apparently the same time. That word is also used in Habakkuk 2:3, Amos 8:2, Ezekiel 7:2–6). Daniel 11:45 is where the King of the North comes to his final end (*qets* is also used in vs. 40 when the King of the North invades the King of the South, which is apparently the end of the King of the South).

Thus, these passages all refer to the same general time period at the end.

They have not been completely fulfilled, despite claims from preterists: these passages need to be understood as prophetic.

Greco-Roman Catholic, Protestant, and other scholars are correct that there was some semi-fulfillment of many of these verses by Antiochus Epiphanes and others, as there is a duality in some prophecies (cf. 1 Corinthians 15:45-47; Jeremiah 23:7-8). However, since the final appointed time has not yet come, these verses specifically do have a final end-time fulfillment.

And the proper place to look for the final fulfillment to begin is no later than verse 27 (though verses also 21-26 seemingly parallel some of the later verses).

So, beginning with Daniel 11:27, with the scriptures in **bold**:

27 Both these kings' hearts *shall be* bent on evil, and they shall speak lies at the same table; but it shall not prosper, for the end *will* still *be* at the appointed time. (NKJV)

27 The heart also of the two Kings shall be to evil, and at one table they shall speak lies, and they shall not prosper: because as yet the end unto another time. (DRB)

The "they" is referring to the kings of the North and South, as they are the kings both later and earlier mentioned in most of Daniel 11.

Verse 27 suggests that some type of bad agreement is made between the two — this would seem to be the deal that leads to the fulfillment of Psalm 83. It is highly likely that this deal will be portrayed publicly as a type of peace deal, but in fact will unleash terror.

In his commentary related to this verse, the Greco-Roman saint Jerome stated his belief "that all these things refer to the Antichrist and to the king of Egypt."[155] Thus the idea that there is a future fulfillment of Daniel 11, starting no later than verse 27, is not simply a modern concept.

Some, including the Jehovah's Witnesses, have correctly taught, "The designations 'the king of the north' and 'the king of the south' refer to kings north and south of Daniel's people ...{in} to the land of Judah."[156] Yet, despite the correct understanding of geography, the Jehovah's Witnesses incorrectly conclude that in the 20th century the United States and the United Kingdom became the King of the South.[157]

Psalm 83 shows those peoples will have decided to destroy Israel and that the descendants of ancient Assyria (which in modern times includes various ones in Europe) will later decide to join them.

Other biblical prophecies indicate that "Israel" includes more than those in the modern nation of Israel (cf. Genesis 48, 49). For now, let us understand that prophetically the

Bible shows that an Arab-Turkish confederation wants to eliminate the descendants of Israel, perhaps through terrorism and warfare, and that the Assyrian (apparently European based on other prophecies) power decides to join them in order for this to succeed.

Verse 27 likely sets the stage for proposing that the Antichrist supporters come to Jerusalem to eliminate Israeli control of that city, as well as to fulfill Daniel 11:31 and probably Daniel 11:39.

Notice that this deal in Daniel 11:27 will be based upon deceit but will result in the end coming **at the appointed time**. Thus, this deal apparently pertains to the appointed time of the end.

Because of that, the Bible clearly supports the idea that *there must be a future fulfillment of verse 27 onwards*. And this deal, (most details of it will likely not be made public), may be the next major prophetic fulfillment and may happen about the same time as the covenant in Daniel 9:27, or possibly after it.

28 While returning to his land with great riches, his heart shall be *moved* against the holy covenant; so he shall do *damage* and return to his own land.

In addition to setting the stage for a prosperous King of the North (see also verse 36 below), the above specifically indicates that something will upset the King of the North, apparently related to a visit to the Palestine/Israel area, and he will return to his land (Europe) upset with the holy covenant, probably the most faithful of spiritual Israel (Romans 9:6).

During the end times, true Christians would seem to have to be the people of the holy covenant (see Matthew 26:28;

Hebrews 8:6–13; Daniel 12:7). Baptism and receiving God's Holy Spirit is what makes one an heir of the "holy covenant" in the New Testament, (cf. Luke 1:72–73 & Galatians 3:26–29; Romans 8:9-11).

The reason that the King of the North may be *moved against* the most faithful Christians is that they may be somewhat effectively reporting/broadcasting what this deal in verses 27 may mean—as well as what is expected to happen next. They may also have tried to expose the deal in Daniel 9:26–27, if it was earlier, as well.

By this time, the short work/word Paul mentioned in Romans 9:28 probably will have begun or be almost finished, as will the gospel preaching of Matthew 24:14 that Jesus spoke of. Both are part of what I have termed "the final phase of the work."

What causes the northern king's heart to be against the holy covenant of the most faithful in God's Church, and what he does then is not specified in Daniel's writings. It should perhaps be noted that the word "damage" is not in the original Hebrew, so perhaps something else may be going on.

For example, the King of the North may simply say something publicly, such as threatening to affect the true *Philadelphia* Christians' (Revelation 3:7-13) ability to continue to broadcast messages such as the gospel of the kingdom of God, a message that is not popular, with many. He could call the message hate speech, a conspiracy theory, fake news, dangerous, and/or whatever he thinks may get his point across.

The *United States Conference of Catholic Bishops* explains:

"The letter to Philadelphia praises the Christians

there for remaining faithful even with their limited strength... they will be kept safe at the great trial ... [3:8] **An open door**: opportunities for sharing and proclaiming the faith."[158]

These end-time *Philadelphia* Christians' are those who go through the open door of Revelation 3:7-8 to proclaim the Gospel (cf. Colossians 4:3) and have truly held fast to biblical teachings (Revelation 13:7-13).

These genuine and most faithful Church of God Christians (Acts 20:28) may have upset the King of the North by telling the world in general, and the Americans in particular, that he is apparently the prophesied King of the North, likely the Great Monarch of Catholic prophecy, and that he will soon invade and destroy Israel and the Anglo-American nations (Daniel 11:31,39) and then an Arabic-Muslim confederation (Daniel 11:40-43).

Notice the following translation of verse 28 in the *Contemporary English Version* (CEV). It supports the view that the holy covenant could be the true Christians at the end, as Christianity, and not Judaism, is now the "religion of God's people." The *Douay-Rheims Bible* as it uses the term "holy testament":

> [28] Then the king of the north will return to his country with great treasures. But on the way, he will attack the religion of God's people and do whatever else he pleases. (CEV)

> [28] And he shall return into his land with much riches: and his heart against the holy testament, and he shall prosper and shall return into his own land. (DRB)

Hence, Daniel 11:28 supports the notion that the true church is the holy covenant/holy testament. Notice also the following rendering of this verse from *The Message* (MSG) translation:

> 28 The king of the north will go home loaded down with plunder, but his mind will be set on destroying the holy covenant as he passes through the country on his way home. (MSG)

There is something intriguing about the above rendering.

It suggests that the King of the North has made up his mind that it is time to destroy the holy covenant, or at least part of the Christian message. He may have decided to begin persecution, interfere with broadcasting/internet abilities, and/or at least began to think of plans to affect these Christians. These actions are likely to begin no later than Daniel 11:30, if one or more does not begin in or by 11:28 (both of which are shortly before the start of the Great Tribulation).

Regardless of the verse that shows when this persecution precisely begins, it is clear that specific persecution will happen through verse 35, and it may include all of the forty-five-day period (1335 days-1290 days), and part of the thirty-day-period (1290 days-1260 days), in Daniel 12:11–12.

This looks to be the time when Satan is cast to the earth. Let us again notice what Revelation 12:13–14 shows:

> 13 Now when the dragon saw that he had been cast to the earth, **he persecuted the woman** who gave birth to the male Child.
>
> 14 But the woman was given two wings of a great eagle, that she might fly into the wilderness to her place, where she is nourished for a time and times and half a time.

117

This persecution appears to mainly be a persecution against the *Philadelphian* Christians (Revelation 3:8), as they are given protection shortly thereafter (Revelation 3:10). Yet it needs to be understood that the woman is apparently still persecuted until verse 16 of Revelation 12, therefore, the persecutions of the Philadelphians apparently occur until Daniel 11:35 — when the archangel Michael may stand (Daniel 12:1), a decree is issued (Zephaniah 2:1-3), and the Philadelphians flee into the wilderness, for protection (Revelation 3:7-10).

Even the *Book of Mormon* speaks of a time when a great kingdom will arise with a great church and persecute:

> And it came to pass that I saw among the nations of the Gentiles the formation of a great church ... which is abominable ... which slays the saints of God, yea and tortureth them ...[159]

Also, notice that the Bible states:

> [6] "Flee from the land of the north," says the LORD ...[7] Up Zion! Escape you that dwell with the daughter of Babylon (Zechariah 2:6, 7).

It may be that prior to going to a place of protection (cf. Revelation 12:13–14), some Christians will flee out of the lands dominated by the rising King of the North prior to him moving into Jerusalem, probably during verses 28–30 of Daniel 11, as this is when the King of the North begins his anger against God's most faithful. Since God's faithful will apparently understand these passages in Daniel 11 by then (cf. Daniel 12:10), some will not wait until verses 30 or 31 to flee from the north, and will most likely go to Judea.

29 At the appointed time he shall return and go toward the south; but it shall not be like the former or the latter.

The 'he' is still the King of the North. This verse suggests that the "appointed time" is not only different than any before, but that **this is the specific appointed time that leads to the final end** of both the King of the North and the King of the South (cf. vs. 27).

Although he had other misunderstandings, even the Protestant commentator, A. Faucett, realized that the deal in Daniel 11:27 is related to the fulfillment in verse 29 as he wrote the following about Daniel 11:29:

> **29. At the time appointed**--"the time" spoken of in Daniel 11:27.[160]

Political interference, with perhaps bringing some troops on ships, is probably what is happening in verse 29 as ships come against this King in the next verse.

30a For ships from Cyprus shall come against him;

According to *Vine's Expository Reference*, the Hebrew term translated as Cyprus above, *kittim*, means "Western lands."[161]

The Catholic Jerome wrote about this as follows:

> *"And his heart shall be against the holy covenant, and he shall succeed and return into his own land. At the time appointed he shall return and shall come to the South; but the latter time shall not be like the former. And the galleys shall come upon him, and the Romans, and he shall be dealt a heavy blow."* Or, as another has rendered it, "... and they shall threaten him with attack."[162]

Daniel 11:30 suggests that a major western naval power will put on a display of force and that will upset the south-heading King of the North, who will then decide to enter at least the area where Jews are making sacrifices, perhaps in retaliation for that action and/or to satisfy the complaints of his King of the South allies (vs. 27). A similar passage is in Numbers 24:24, which according to Numbers 24:14, is clearly for the latter times—and in it, the Western naval power troubles descendants of Asshur/Assyria, many of whom now are residing in Europe.

It is of interest to note that the U.S.A. and its ships, from a Judean or European Union perspective, are from western lands.

Of course, it is also possible that the U.S.A. or some other country could have naval ships in Cyprus or some other western land. However, **no small country with a minor naval presence would be likely to stop the King of the North at that stage of history—thus the U.S.A. (perhaps with some of its allies) seems to be the only possible naval force mentioned here**.

Note: *Because the nation of Cyprus, and many other western European countries, are part of the European Union, we have to eliminate them as being part of the "Western lands" in Daniel 11. Furthermore, since the Kings of the East and North are not alluded to until Daniel 11:44, we have to eliminate Russia, China, India, and Japan as possible naval forces for verse 30 (plus, of course, those nations are east and north, not west of Jerusalem).*

Also, because the Arab nations would tend to be supporters of the King of the South, there is no nation in an actual "western" area that this could possibly refer to in the early 21st century other than the U.S.A., Canada, the Caribbean, or Latin America.

And neither Latin America, nor the non-Spanish Caribbean countries, seem capable, at this point, of having a naval force that would stop the King of the North. Thus, watching and understanding current world events, as Jesus advised, (e.g. Mark 13:32-37) makes it clear that the naval power would have to be the U.S.A. and possibly also include its English-speaking allies.

Canadian and American Warships

Here is the entire verse 30 from 3 different translations: the *Bible in Basic English* (BBE), GOD'S WORD® Translation ©1995 (GWT), NJB, and the CEV:

> For those who go out from the west will come against him, and he will be in fear and will go back, full of wrath against the holy agreement; and he will do his pleasure: and he will go back and be united with those who have given up the holy agreement. (BBE)

> Ships will come from the west to attack him, and he will be discouraged and turn back. Angry at the holy promise, he will return, take action, and favor those who abandon the holy promise. (GWT)

> The ships of the Kittim will oppose him, and he will be worsted. He will retire and take furious action against the holy covenant and, as before, will favour those who forsake that holy covenant. (NJB)

> Ships from the west will come to attack him, and he will

be discouraged. Then he will start back to his own country and take out his anger on the religion of God's faithful people, while showing kindness to those who are unfaithful. (CEV)

Notice that the ships, while they may come to attack, do not have to actually attack the King of the North at this time — and that they seem to come from "the west."

But also notice that instead of taking his anger out against the naval power that sends the ships, the King of the North takes out his anger against what scripture looks to suggest is *the religion of God's faithful people!*

It seems obvious that these are the faithful Christians who are doing the main specific end-time work of God at this time. And they will be explaining these prophecies to the world.

About five years after I first thought that Daniel 11:30 could be referring to United States warships, I came across the following in a book written about Greco-Roman prophecies by Gerald Culleton:

> *Countess Francesca de Billiante* (died 1935): When the land with the great fleet enters the Mediterranean (England or the United States?) then Europe will tremble … God will save Rome …[163]

The comments in ( ) are from the late Roman Catholic priest and writer Gerald Culleton.

Because the Bible shows that the spirit world has knowledge of scripture (Matthew 4:5–6), it would appear that some spirits inspired this and certain private prophets to make a variety of statements throughout history to try to confuse people at the end (cf. 1 Timothy 4:1; 2 Corinthians

2:11). The statement from the Countess may have been intended to tell the Europeans that they should not be too afraid of the coming "American" ships.

While Priest Culleton did not connect this prediction to Daniel 11:30 in his writing, notice the following by Roman priest, Professor P. Huchedé, that connects that verse to Western naval forces:

> It seems he will probably be defeated by certain people of the Western nations, who will give him a naval battle … (11:30). But he will soon recover from this defeat.[164]

When this event happens, all should realize that it is showing that Daniel 11:30, etc. is being fulfilled. The King of the North and his allies will not want people to believe this.

THIS WILL BE A MAJOR SIGN FOR PEOPLE WHO WILL PAY ATTENTION AND HEED THAT THE END (the start of the Great Tribulation) IS VERY NEAR.

30b therefore he shall be grieved, and return in rage against the holy covenant, and do *damage.*

Partially because the U.S. naval forces have stopped him AND the most faithful Christians are causing the modified ecumenical religion problems (as the media is likely to report much more of the Philadelphian Church's message then), the King of the North will decide to do something to the members of the true Church ("damage" is not in the Hebrew) after he returns. This would be because he is "in rage against **the holy covenant.**"

Around the late fourth century, Jerome taught about this portion of verse:

... foreshadows the Antichrist, who is to persecute the people of Christ.[165]

The King of the North will most likely try to stop the supporters of the true church from proclaiming the truth about his intentions and from proclaiming "the gospel of the kingdom" (cf. Matthew 24:14) — which will be in opposition to his message. In the past several years, many in Europe and elsewhere have taken steps to be able to censor internet content, and some of that looks to be prophesied to happen.

It continues to strike me as important that although a western naval power stops the King of the North momentarily, **the King of the North becomes seemingly more enraged with the people of the holy covenant than with the naval power**. He wants to eliminate the rising up of what some Greco-Roman prophecies call the "secret sect"![166]

Why would this be?

Most likely this occurs because the people of the holy covenant ("secret sect") are warning the world that the King of the North is fulfilling these prophecies in Daniel 11. This enrages the King of the North so much that he tries to eliminate these people. The King of the North simply does not want the small continuing faithful Church telling the world in general, or the Anglo-Saxon-American nations in particular, what some of his plans really are. Perhaps he also thinks that his relationship with the then U.S.A. president is still close enough that he has enough influence to push his censorship.

Jesus clearly taught that persecution would affect His people just prior to the beginning of the Great Tribulation:

7 And there will be famines, pestilences, and earthquakes in various places. 8 All these are **the beginning of sorrows**. 9 Then **they will deliver you up to tribulation and kill you**, and you will be hated by all nations for My name's sake. 10 And then many will be offended, will betray one another, and will hate one another (Matthew 24:7-10).

14 And this gospel of the kingdom will be preached in all the world as a witness to all the nations, and then the end will come. 15 "Therefore when you see the 'abomination of desolation,' spoken of by Daniel the prophet, standing in the holy place" (whoever reads, let him understand), 16 then let those who are in Judea flee to the mountains...21 For **then there will be great tribulation** (Matthew 24:14-16;21).

So, notice that after the sorrows have begun, faithful Christians will be delivered up. Many will be killed, and many will be betrayed by those pretending to be Christians. Christ's "gospel of the kingdom is preached to the world as a witness," then the GREAT tribulation will come shortly thereafter. This clearly ties in with the events of Daniel 11, as Jesus Himself seemed to tie Daniel 11:31 into Matthew 24:15.

This may be precisely when God has the work of His Philadelphia remnant church, in a more organized manner, stopped (Romans 9:28; Amos 8:11) — perhaps getting kicked off electronic media, probably including the internet. However, at least parts of the message will apparently continue to go out by scattered and fleeing individuals, as well as the two witnesses. It may be (and this is certainly speculative) that the Americans agree to stop (or pressure or suspend on some pretext) the faithful church's ability to boldly proclaim the message as part of the negotiations that certainly will be needed because of the encounter between the King of the North (Europe) and the naval forces of the West (America).

Part b of verse 30 appears to parallel Matthew 24:9–10. This indicates that some type of persecution of true Christians will begin before the "gospel of the kingdom" will have gone to the world as witness, as that is completed in Matthew 24:14. Notice that the end comes once the Christians have successfully proclaimed the "gospel of the kingdom." This success would have been attained with inadvertent assistance through media coverage.

It is possible that verse 30b is when the two witnesses officially appear with power (or perhaps in or between vss. 31–39), as they will undoubtedly enrage the King of the North—of course so will the faithful Christians who do the work.

30c So he shall return and show regard for those who forsake the holy covenant.

It is somewhat possible that "those who **forsake** the holy covenant" are former "Christians," who in that sense have actually forsaken the biblical covenant.

Perhaps this includes those involved in the falling away (see 2 Thessalonians 2:3). The reason that the King of the North may wish to show them some type of favor may be so the King can learn more about the Christians to better be able to identify, eliminate, and/or persecute its followers. His plan is to get them to betray the faithful Christians (cf. Matthew 24:10).

Here is what Jerome taught about the fulfillment of this portion of the verse:

… this is to be more amply fulfilled under the Antichrist, for he shall become angered at the covenant of God and devise plans against those whom he wishes to forsake the law of God.[167]

The Beast and the Antichrist will be against the law of God (for details, check out the free book, available online at ccog.org titled *The Ten Commandments: The Decalogue, Christianity, and the Beast*).

Notice that Jesus listed betrayal just before the abomination of Daniel is mentioned:

> [12] Now brother will betray brother to death, and a father his child; and children will rise up against parents and cause them to be put to death. [13] And you will be hated by all men for My name's sake. But he who endures to the end shall be saved.
>
> [14] "So when you see the 'abomination of desolation,' spoken of by Daniel the prophet, standing where it ought not" (let the reader understand), "then let those who are in Judea flee to the mountains" (Mark 13:12-14).

Thus, it appears that Daniel is referring to a betrayal—a deliverance to persecuting authorities—by supposed believers and/or the members of their physical family. In Matthew 24:10 Jesus also makes a similar warning.

31 And forces shall be mustered by him, and they shall defile the sanctuary fortress; then they shall take away the daily *sacrifices*, and place *there* the abomination of desolation.

The above verse shows that the forces of the King of the North will stop the daily sacrifices. Of course, for the daily sacrifices to stop, they will have had to start—thus this is a prophetic event that one can watch for (cf. Matthew 24:15; Luke 21:20). Since December 10, 2018, certain Jews claim to have a Sanhedrin dedicated altar to do that. [168]

While the term "sacrifices" is not in the original Hebrew, Daniel 9:27 mentions what appears to be the same desolate abominations, and also the Hebrew shows that the sacrifices and offerings will be stopped. It may be that part of the reason the King of the North will give for going into Jerusalem with armies is to stop extremists from having daily sacrifices that may provoke the Muslims and others.

Interestingly, this starting of sacrifices in Israel might be perceived as the terrible crime that a Roman Catholic long ago prophesied would lead to some type of destruction:

> *Abbot Herman of Lehnin* (died 1300) Towards the end of the world "Israel will commit a terrible crime for which it will suffer death."[169]

In these days, because of 'animal rights' and Islamic influences, animal sacrifices may be perceived to be a terrible crime. On the other hand, the Bible tells of the destruction of Damascus (Isaiah 17:1), and the nation of Israel may be involved in that or something involving Iran.

Unlike in Daniel 11:30, the King of the North meets no strong naval resistance in verse 31. This may be because he negotiated something with the U.S.A. to allow him (possibly with an "antipope") to go to Jerusalem to broker/enforce some kind of "peace in the Middle East."

Yet, it is likely that the King of the North will do things that he had not told the U.S.A. he would do; such as go after the Philadelphian Christians and interfere with Jewish practices and/or politics.

This may then inflame the U.S.A. enough (as it may feel at least partially betrayed) that it may be one of the reasons that the King of the North decides on a "blitzkrieg" invasion of the U.S.A. and/or its British-descended allies 30 days after stopping the daily sacrifices. The fact that the Europeans could be controlling at least part of the U.S.A.'s global positioning capabilities within the next decade[170] (the related agreement of which happened under the Obama-Biden Administration) may be enough to embolden the King, especially once he has developed other weapons' technology.

This King will employ deceit:

> [21] ... he shall come in peaceably, and seize the kingdom by intrigue. (Daniel 11:21)

> [23] "And in the latter time of their kingdom, When the transgressors have reached their fullness, A king shall arise, Having fierce features, Who understands sinister schemes. [24] His power shall be mighty, but not by his own power; He shall destroy fearfully, And shall prosper and thrive; He shall destroy the mighty, and also the holy people.

> [25] "Through his cunning he shall cause deceit to prosper under his rule; And he shall exalt himself in his heart. He shall destroy many in their prosperity. (Daniel 8:23-25)

The King of the North will deceitfully proclaim "peace and safety" while plotting for the sudden destruction of those opposing him (1 Thessalonians 5:2–3). Some political and other leaders will be hoping for and believing in a false peace. The sudden destruction to come is likely to include a nuclear or other high tech attack, and could possibly happen in conjunction with a NATO training or other exercise that would catch the U.S.A. and its Anglo-Saxon allies off guard. Other nations are likely to also be involved.

Doesn't the following sound like nuclear destruction?

> [23] 'The whole land is brimstone, salt, and burning; it is not sown, nor does it bear, nor does any grass grow there, **like the overthrow of Sodom and Gomorrah**, Admah, and Zeboiim, which the Lord overthrew in His anger and His wrath.' [24] All nations would say, 'Why has the Lord done so to this land? What does the heat of this great anger mean?' [25] Then people would say: 'Because they have forsaken the covenant of the Lord God of their fathers … (Deuteronomy 29:23-25)

God destroyed Sodom and Gomorrah for their pride and sexual immorality (Ezekiel 16:49-50; 2 Peter 2:6).

What will happen to the Anglo-lands will actually be worse than what happened to Sodom:

> [6] The punishment of the iniquity of the daughter of my people Is greater than the punishment of the sin of Sodom, Which was overthrown in a moment, With no hand to help her! (Lamentations 4:6)

Like many political leaders, Joe Biden and Kamala Harris have endorsed/condoned aspects of sexual immorality that the Bible condemns.

The time will come when the U.S.A. and NATO will be no more. NATO or other arrangements will give the Europeans cover for publicly preparing for a military event, while giving it the ability to publicly state that such preparations are only parts of an exercise. The Germans have historically used the element of surprise to gain military advantage — remember WWII and blitzkrieg?

130

Europe one day will turn on the U.S.A. (Lamentations 1:1-2, Daniel 11:39; Isaiah 10:5-12).

According to Greco-Roman private prophecies, the Great Monarch, apparently with his forces, is expected to go to Jerusalem toward the beginning and again at end of his reign and fight:

> *Y. Dupont* (20th century): The Great King will be of Frankish descent, although his actual nationality is uncertain...It seems that he will travel twice to Jerusalem, once at the beginning of his reign...and again at the end to fight... and be killed...[171]

> *Helen Otto Tzima* (2000): Jerusalem will be invaded in WWIII and finally liberated by the Great Monarch.[172]

Interestingly, a pope that does miracles and who works with the Great Monarch ("the Beast") is expected to "recover the kingdom of Jerusalem" according to a 12th century Greco-Roman prophecy.[173]

If the final Antichrist, probably some type of "antipope," moves to Jerusalem to aid "world peace" (such as related to the Jewish/Palestinian situation), it would seem to make sense that he comes to Jerusalem prior to the King of the South fighting the King of the North (Daniel 11:40). This move may give the Arab world major cause for concern. Jesus warned of a coming time when Jerusalem would be "surrounded by armies" (Luke 21:20) and "trampled by Gentiles" (vs.24), which parallels a similar warning in Revelation 11:2.

The Bible says an abomination will be set up in "the holy place" in Jerusalem by supporters of the Beast. Daniel 11:31, is the signal for the Philadelphians to flee per Jesus' comments in Matthew 24:15–16 and Revelation 3:10 prior to the start of the Great Tribulation (Matthew 24:21).

Even *The Catholic Encyclopedia* seems to tie Jesus' statements in Matthew 24:15 to Daniel 11:31. However, it is somewhat unclear about what that connection actually means.[174]

32 Those who do wickedly against the covenant he shall corrupt with flattery; but the people who know their God shall be strong, and carry out *great exploits.*

"Those who do wickedly against the covenant" would appear to be those who persecute/harm the faithful church (those of "the covenant"), the other nations that support the King of the North—possibly former Christians who forsook the truth—and/or perhaps some of the Laodicean Christians (Revelation 3:14-21). If so, this could represent a major separation between the Philadelphians and the Laodiceans (who are lukewarm Christians)—which must happen close to that time. Many will betray brethren (cf. Mark 13:21).

Here is the *Douay Rheim's* translation and related comments on this verse:

> [32] And the impious against the testament shall dissemble fraudulently: but ([m]) the people that knoweth their God, shall obtain, and shall doe.
>
> ([m]) even in the hottest persecution of Antiochus, Nero or Antichrist some shall constantly confess true religion.[175]

It is likely that the Philadelphian Christians (Revelation 3:7-13) are the ones who are strong and will carry out something important.

The 19ᵗʰ century Methodist theologian Adam Clarke, in his commentary, identifies the people as follows:

> *But the people that do know their God*
> The genuine Christians.
>
> *Shall be strong*
> Shall be strengthened by his grace and Spirit.[176]

The words *great exploits* in the NKJV do not literally appear in the Hebrew text. The NJB says that they will "take action." Perhaps these faithful Christians will display the types of miraculous signs that Jesus mentioned in Mark 16:15–18, Peter in Acts 2:17-18, and/or the Apostle Paul in 1 Corinthians 12:1-11. These people truly know their God, keep the word of Christ, and have works that are approved, and thus are Philadelphian Christians—as the Bible states of the Philadelphian Christians:

> [8] I know your works. See, I have set before you an open door, and no one can shut it; for you have a little strength, have kept My word, and have not denied My name (Revelation 3:8).

Joel 2:28–31 also suggests a future fulfillment of Daniel 11:32 as those prophesying then may be part of those who are strong and who carry out the exploits and these may occur when the Philadelphians are somewhat fleeing (cf. Revelation 12:14-17).

11:33 And those of the people who understand shall instruct many; yet *for many* days they shall fall by sword and flame, by captivity and plundering.

Those who **understand and instruct many** are those who faithfully do the work of God. This would seem to mainly be the Philadelphia portion of the Church. Some will be killed and will also possibly have their houses or other buildings burned down.

This may occur for a relatively short period of time. It needs to be understood that the expression "for many" is not in the Hebrew before the word "days." The MKJV (Modern King James Version), the LITV (Literal Translation of the Holy Bible), and also the DRB did a better job with this verse as shown below:

> [33] And those who understand among the people shall teach many; yet they shall fall by the sword, and by flame, by exile, and spoil, for days. (Daniel 11:33, MKJV)

> [33] And those who understand among *the* people will instruct many, yet they will stumble by the sword and by flame, by exile and spoil *for* days. (Daniel 11:33, LITV)

> [33] And the learned in the people shall teach very many: and they shall fall by sword, and by flame, and by captivity, and by spoil of days. (Daniel 11:33, DRB)

Thus, there will be some **days** where intense persecution of the Philadelphian Christians will occur *before* they all flee and later receive supernatural protection from God, through His angels.

Regarding falling by the flame, there is also a Roman Catholic,[177] as well as a Byzantine,[178] prophecy that indicates members of a small sect will be burnt, possibly in at least partial fulfillment of this verse.

34 Now when they fall, they shall be aided with a little help; but many shall join with them by intrigue.

Verse 34 further suggests that some Philadelphians will suffer, as it is the Philadelphians that should be those of high understanding.

It should be pointed out that those suffering *may* be the Philadelphians (and/or other Christians) in areas controlled or influenced by the King of the North, specifically Europe, and possibly also includes Latin America. It may be that there will be a religious resurgence (cf. Revelation 13:4,8) that leads to some of God's people being killed in those lands, and even the U.S.A., etc., by self-appointed vigilantes calling themselves "Catholic" (such as one who actually called for a real crusade to begin in the 21st century). [179]

Those who join with the Philadelphia or other Christians by intrigue may include those having fallen away or others pretending to assist the Christians, yet secretly really supporting the King of the North. Greek Orthodox scholar H. Tzima Otto believes that some claiming Philadelphia Christian practices (she does not use the term "Philadelphia Christians," but instead calls them Sabbatians, meaning seventh-day Sabbath-keepers) are going to betray genuine Philadelphians in the future and support the Great Monarch.[180]

Daniel 11:34 is a warning to the end-time Christians that while some will actually help them then, they will need to be quite cautious, as problems are likely with "many."

35 And some of those of understanding shall fall, to refine them, purify them, and make them white, until the time of the end; because it is still for the appointed time.

Verse 35 further shows problems for many of the most faithful in the Church. Because not even the faithful are perfect, some apparently will fall and/or be persecuted, so that they can be refined (spiritually improved).

But Daniel 12:1 shows that this specific persecution will probably end in, or shortly after, verse 35. Then, probably by the beginning of Daniel 11:39 at the latest, the great tribulation will begin.

Why?

The expression translated as "the appointed time" in verse 35 is from the Hebrew word transliterated into English as `eth.[181] It is used in both Daniel 12:1 and 11:35.

The same Hebrew word (`eth) is translated as "the set time" in Psalm 102:13:

> [13] You will arise and have mercy on Zion; For
> the time to favor her, Yes, the set time, has come.

This seems to show that these verses (Daniel 11:35 and Psalm 102:13) are for the same time. If so, this is the time when God distinguishes between the truly faithful Church (called "Zion" above), and those outside the most faithful Church (cf. Revelation 12:13-17). Perhaps this is a parallel to when God no longer had the children of Israel experience the plagues in Egypt, while the Egyptians did (Exodus 8:22).

However, one thing that is critical to notice is that verse 35 specifically shows that its activities go "until the time of the end"—**thus there must be a future fulfillment of vs. 35. And this may be a key verse to tie in with Daniel 12:1**.

The Wycliffe Bible Commentary supports that view (**bolding** in original):

Dan 12:1

At that time (cf. on Dan 11:36). At the same time as the events of 11:36–45. **Michael**. See Rev 12:7; cf. Josh 5:13–15; 2 Kings 6:15–17; Isa 37:35–36; Matt 26:53. This is Israel's time of trouble. Every reference to it uses superlative language (cf. also Matt 24:21).[182]

Yet, the above from *The Wycliffe Bible Commentary* is off a little bit.

Why?

Because the same Hebrew expression for "at that time" (`*eth*) occurs in verse 35, *not* verse 36. Anyway, somewhere between verse 35 and 39 is apparently when Michael stands up and begins to protect the Philadelphians.

The Philadelphians apparently will flee during vs. 35, as Jesus said that His people would flee just prior to the great tribulation in Matthew 24:20–21. Jesus specified that they would escape in Luke 21:36. Jesus stated that it would be the Philadelphians who would be kept "from the hour of trial which shall come upon the whole world" in Revelation 3:10.

The Bible shows that persecution will accompany this fleeing (Revelation 12:13–15), but that those fleeing are helped (vs. 16). Because of the successful fleeing, the King of the North will stop his direct pursuit of them. The faithful will no longer be proclaiming the gospel through any major organized media effort (cf. Amos 8:11-12). The rising up of the "secret sect" some Greco-Roman writings allude to will have ended.

Greco-Roman prophecies seem to foretell this time and the Philadelphian "sect" will apparently be perceived to be the enemy of the Great Monarch and the antipope:

St. Francis of Paola (Born in Italy, 15th century): the Great Monarch will annihilate heretics and unbelievers ... All in all, there will be on earth twelve Kings, one Emperor, one Pope and a few Princes.[183]

David Poreus (17th century): The Great Monarch...will crush the enemies of the Pope ...[184]

Thus, as far as most will be concerned, the faithful Christians will have been "crushed" as heretics.

The Faithful Philadelphians May Dwell in Caves

Many theologians, consistent with Revelation 12:14-16, have considered that part of the true Church would flee into the wilderness during this time[185]; and others specifically believe that this place has caves.[186]

The late Protestant Dr. Tim LaHaye referred to a mountainous cave-filled place in Jordan called Petra (shown on the back cover of this book in the print edition) and the people who flee as "believing Jews."[187]

It would seem that those called "believing Jews" (historically, sometimes known as Nazarene Christians) represent the faithful sect that certain mystics have improperly warned about. Philadelphian, like other real, Christians have some practices considered "Jewish" as Revelation 3:7-9 and 2:9 suggests. The fact that Jesus told His followers, to "pray that your flight may not be in winter or on the Sabbath" (Matthew 24:20) also confirms this. The Bible is clear that at the time of the fleeing, even those who do not flee, but are to be persecuted "keep the commandments of God and have the testimony of Jesus Christ" (Revelation 12:17).

However, at least one mystic warned in the 12th century that while those in caves seemed to be good, she felt they really were not:

> *Hildegard of Bingen* (12th century): And fly from those who linger in caves and are cloistered supporters of the Devil. Woe to them, woe to them who remain thus! They are the Devil's very viscera, and the advance guard of the son of perdition.
>
> Therefore, O you My beloved children, avoid them with all devotion and with all the strength of your souls and bodies. For the ancient serpent feeds and clothes them by his arts, and they worship him as God and trust in his false deceptions...Because they are afraid of My people, they do not openly resist these institutions of Mine, but in their hearts and their deeds they hold them as nothing. By devilish illusion, they pretend to have sanctity; but they are deceived by the Devil, for if he were to show himself to them openly they would understand him and flee him…But because the Devil knows he has only a short time for his error, he is not hastening to perfect infidelity in his members; you, you evil deceivers, who labor to subvert the Catholic faith.[188]

It would appear that the mystic was demonically-influenced as she is actually warning against supporting the true Philadelphian pacifist Christians (something that may happen, as some not originally with them might try to join them per Isaiah 56:8).

It is the Philadelphians who will be protected, yet she seems to be claiming that they are the "supporters of the Devil" (probably because they will oppose the final revised ecumenical church and because that church will have persecuted them). Because she calls them "the advanced guard of the son of perdition," she apparently refers to a group of people who will be protected in caves just before Christ returns.

Notice also that she specifically warns against religious people in caves who are miraculously fed.

Yet, she must not have realized that the Bible indicates that those who receive God's protection in the wilderness during the end time (Revelation 12:14–16), and are in caves (Jeremiah 48:28), are His people (Isaiah 16:1–4 possibly in Sela/Petra), will be religious (Revelation 14:12), and will be miraculously fed (Isaiah 33:15-16). Hence, the above vision does support the view that even the demons have understood about a place of protection where some people will be miraculously fed, for quite some time.

However, those associated with the King of the North will then turn their attention to the rest of her seed, the non-Philadelphian Christians (who will be a kind of "secret sect" but will try to remain hidden, most likely to avoid this persecution).

Even a commentator's note in the *Rheims New Testament* agrees that the Church goes to a wilderness location:

> The Church shall flee as to a desert in Antichrist's time, but not decay or be unknown, no not for so short a time. [189]

Early Greco-Roman "fathers" such as Irenaeus,[190] Hippolytus,[191] and Cyril[192] also believed this. Hence Hildegard is once again not even faithful to Greco-Roman Catholic positions on prophetic matters.
Furthermore, notice:

Bishop St. Victorinus (2nd century): But the woman fled into the wilderness, and there were given to her two great eagle's wings … to that … church … let them go to that place which they have ready, and let them be supported there for three years and six months from the presence of the devil.[193]

Thus, the idea of true Christians fleeing, being supported, and being away from the devil for 3 ½ years is consistent with both biblical and certain Roman Catholic teachings.[194]

No one should rely on Hildegard's false admonition. The Greek Orthodox also tend to believe that the faithful will flee to caves in the desert/wilderness for 3 ½ years.[195]

Now, it should be understood that the Bible shows that those who do not flee then will be persecuted:

> [17] And the dragon was enraged with the woman, and he went to make war with the rest of her offspring, who keep the commandments of God and have the testimony of Jesus Christ (Revelation 12:17).

Thus, we see several parallels in Daniel 11:29–35 and Revelation 12:13–17. We specifically see that some will be persecuted, will flee to the wilderness, will be helped, but that Satan is not yet through (as Daniel 11:36-44 also seem to show).

The Spanish-influenced 16th century Mayan *Chilam Balam* warns that those associated with a church will be in a cave:

> Son, where is the cenote? All are drenched <with> its water. There is no gravel on its bottom; a bow is inserted over its entrance. <It is> the church.[196]

The 1933 compiler of the above (J. José Hoíl) added a note stating, "Evidently a reference to a cave type of cenote."[197]

Thus, this Mayan writing is showing the church being in a cave and being drenched with water in a way seemingly consistent with the concept of fleeing to a wilderness and avoiding the flood as shown in Revelation 12:14-16.

36 "Then the king shall do according to his own will: he shall exalt and magnify himself above every god, shall speak blasphemies against the God of gods, and shall prosper till the wrath has been accomplished; for what has been determined shall be done.

The King of the North will prosper and honor his own god, but himself the most. Although there have been partial fulfillments in the past, **this would have to be at the time of the end.**

The prospering in Daniel 11:36 may also be related to Ezekiel 27. If so, this would suggest that the European Union will start prospering through trading before it begins to prosper through military conquest. Notice something that the late evangelist John Ogwyn wrote:

> This European union of church and state will promise universal prosperity and will exercise worldwide economic dominance for a short while. Ezekiel 27, using the figure of the ancient commercial city of Tyre, speaks of this global economic combine which will include nations of Europe, Africa, Latin America, and Asia along with Israel and Judah (v. 17). Portions of Ezekiel 27 are paraphrased or quoted in Revelation 18 where the end-time system, called Babylon the Great, is described.

The English-speaking nations will not prosper for long in connection with this system, however. In fact, they will ultimately be overpowered and destroyed by it militarily. Prior to military attack and occupation, devastating weather problems, combined with internal civil strife ("tumults in the midst" cf. Amos 3:9) will bring our nations to the point of internal collapse.[198]

Thus, a major trading power will prosper. Even today, the European Union is a major trading power.

It should be noted that the term translated as "Then" in vs. 36 (and the "Thus" in vs. 39) is the Hebrew word `asah which according to the *Interlinear Transliterated Bible* actually means "And shall do."[199] Therefore, it may be that every act listed is not necessarily consecutive, as some (from vs. 31 to 39) may be fairly concurrent.

37 He shall regard neither the God of his fathers nor the desire of women, nor regard any god; for he shall exalt himself above *them* all. 38 But in their place he shall honor a god of fortresses; and a god which his fathers did not know he shall honor with gold and silver, with precious stones and pleasant things.

Notice that the King of the North, the ten-horned beast, will really worship himself, but will outwardly honor some type of god, perhaps including technology related to war.

Regarding "any god" in verse 37, it will probably be that the King of the North will pretend to be some type of "Catholic" until it is no longer convenient. The Beast will turn on an unfaithful church later as shown in Revelation 17:16–17.

Let us look at the original KJV here, as it seems a bit truer to the Hebrew intent. The NKJV gives a different impression:

> [37] Neither shall he regard the God of his fathers, nor the desire of women, nor regard any god: for he shall magnify himself above all. [38] But in his estate shall he honour the God of forces: and a god whom his fathers knew not shall he honour with gold, and silver, and with precious stones, and pleasant things (Daniel 11:37–38, KJV).

The word translated both times as "regard" in 11:37 is the Hebrew word *biyn,* which essentially means to have intellectual understanding/perception of.[200]

Essentially, the King of the North will probably consider that the changed 'Catholic' religion should not be taken seriously internally, although, he will at first honor many of its beliefs publicly. Like Emperor Constantine did, he will probably understand that religion may be useful for political purposes, including, at first, keeping the revised Holy Roman Empire united.

Verse 38 looks to be referring to two gods. The god that his fathers did not know (possibly called the foreign god of the next verse) and the god of fortresses. It would seem that those who believe that those who profess Christ, but endorse Christians fighting in carnal warfare, are in a real sense honoring the "god of fortresses." Yet, this is something that the original Nazarene Christians (cf. Acts 24:5) and their true spiritual descendants have never done.

39 Thus he shall act against the strongest fortresses with a foreign god, which he shall acknowledge, and advance its glory; and he shall cause them to rule over many, and divide the land for gain.

The "he" is the King of the North. The two Hebrew words translated as "the strongest fortresses" in verse 39 do not appear together anywhere else in the Bible.

Something is, thus, unique here. Notice another translation which is similar:

> [39] Claiming this foreign god's help, he will attack the strongest fortresses. He will honor those who submit to him, appointing them to positions of authority and dividing the land among them as their reward. (Daniel 11:39, New Living Translation, 2007)

Who has the strongest fortresses?

Looking further down in this chapter in Daniel, we must eliminate the King of the South, because that King is not attacked until later (the next verse). We must also eliminate those in the North and East, as they do not get involved until later (verse 44).

Neither the rest of Africa nor Latin America has anything resembling "the strongest fortresses." The strongest fortresses belong to the United States, and to a much lesser degree, its English-speaking allies. Thus, in current times, Daniel 11:39 looks to be describing when the Anglo-English-American nations are being destroyed.

Catholic Prophecies about the Great Monarch and the Destruction of the English Peoples

Interestingly, there seem to be several Roman Catholic private prophecies that also foretell the destruction of the English-speaking peoples.

It should be noted, however, that many of the older Roman Catholic prophecies that mention the "English" were written before that area actually was called England, but was made up of territories of Anglo-Saxon peoples. Of course, if any apply to the U.S.A., Canada, Australia, and/or New Zealand, they were not formed as we now understand them until several centuries after some of the Roman Catholic prophecies were first written. Hence, although there are errors or distortions in translations, they do seem to somehow refer to the British-American descended peoples. It would seem that they basically were intended to refer to the Anglo-Saxon-American nations in the twenty-first century as they were not fulfilled in previous centuries.

The following Roman Catholic "private prophecies" appear to predict the destruction of the English:

> *St. Columbkille* (597): English nobility shall sink into horrible life—wars shall be proclaimed against them, by means of which the frantically proud race shall be subdued, and will be harassed from every quarter. **The English shall dwindle into disreputable people and shall forever be deprived of power**".[201] ... **the English shall be defeated ... they shall be harassed by every quarter**; like a fawn surrounded by a pack of voracious hounds, shall be the position of the English amidst their enemies. The English afterwards shall dwindle down to a disreputable people.[202]

> *Mother Shipton* (died 1551): The time will come when England shall tremble and quake ... **London shall be destroyed forever after** ... and then York shall be London and the Kingdom governed by three Lords appointed by a Royal Great monarch...who will set England right and drive out heresy.[203]

Saint Edward (died 1066): **The extreme corruption and wickedness of the English nation has provoked the just anger of God**. When malice shall have reached the fullness of its measure, God will, in His wrath, send to the English people wicked spirits, who will punish and afflict them with great severity ...[204]

Saint Malachy (12th century): the English in turn must suffer severe chastisement. Ireland, however, will be instrumental in bringing back the English to the unity of Faith.[205]

Saint Cataldus of Tarentino (c. 500): **The Great Monarch** will be in war till he is forty years of age...he will assemble great armies and expel tyrants from his empire. He **will conquer England** and other island empires.[206]

Franciscan Friar of Mount Sinai (died 1840): England will become the scene of the greatest cruelties. **Ireland and Scotland will invade England and destroy it**. The royal family will be driven out and half of the population murdered.[207]

D.A. Birch (20th century writer): It is interesting to note that the National (Government) of England is foretold to have no role in the return of England to Roman allegiance. As a matter of fact, a number of prophecies specifically state that England will be reevangelized by the French and Irish **after England has suffered a terrible and specific chastisement**.[208]

Priest Paul Kramer (2010): Zachary the Armenian Jew who converted to the Catholic Faith – published in 1854...there would be the war that the prophecy refers to as "the struggle of the strong, against the strong". This empire of the north...will go to war against North America and North America will fall and be conquered and brought into bondage ...[209]

Werdin d' Otrante (13th century): "The Great Monarch and the Great Pope will precede Antichrist ... **All the sects will vanish. The capital of the world will fall** ... The Great Monarch will come and restore peace and the Pope will share in the victory.[210]

In a sense, the capital of the world is the United States. Hence it seems to be the U.S.A. that Werdin d' Otrante was referring to. Notice that Zachary said there would be a battle against the strong of North America by the empire of the north. Thus, certain Roman Catholic prophecies appear to be foretelling the destruction of the Anglo-Saxon-American powers, apparently by their Great Monarch.

Sadly, some may well point to these non-Divinely inspired writings as partial justification for destroying the United States and peoples of some of the other British-descended lands.

It is interesting to note that the Roman Catholic Saint Edward specifically states that demons will be used to punish the English peoples (whether the majority of Scots, etc, will be specifically involved or not can be debated). This would suggest, that presuming that the Great Monarch attacks them, the Great Monarch is on the side of demons. And while this is consistent with scriptures that show that the final ten-horned beast leader is influenced by demons (Revelation 16:13–14), it should give all who call themselves Roman Catholic (and others) pause to NOT support someone who is on the side of demons.

A Greek Orthodox document known as the *Anonymou Paraphrasis* of 1053 also seems to foretell of a time that the

Anglos will no longer be in the area of England,[211] but that nation was not known by that name at that time so it is not clear what is meant by it.

There also was a prophecy from a famous stigmatic (a mystic with blood wounds supposedly reflective of those that Jesus suffered when nailed to the stake):

> *Therese Neumann* (20th century): … at the end of this century America will be destroyed economically by natural disasters. [212]

Although the timing of that prophecy was false, it should be clear according to a variety of sources claiming Catholicism, the United States and the other English-descended peoples are facing disaster—and apparently relatively soon.

While many evangelical Protestants correctly teach that the U.S.A. will be gone before Jesus' second coming (i.e. Hal Lindsey), they generally do not seem to understand how that will happen nor what scripture most clearly refers to this.[213]

Why America and its Anglo-Saxon Allies?

Why would Europe ultimately destroy the U.S.A. and its Anglo-Saxon allies?

There are several reasons.

One would seem to be because it is the, nominally Protestant (as well as religiously diverse/independent), U.S.A. that most stands in the way of the goals of a future single ecumenical religion in Europe to dominate the world.

Only by eliminating the vast bastions of Protestantism and other "heresies" (which several other Greco-Roman prophecies seem to show is a goal) that are present in the U.S.A. and its Anglo-Saxon allies, can such an ecumenical domination be attained in those lands.

Notice what one Roman Catholic priest has written:

> *Priest G. Rossi* (19th century): But boastful pride and presumption always go before a fall. With her large share of guilt, America cannot avoid her due share of punishment...If the world is not yet entirely converted to Christianity, the blame is not on the head nor in the conscience of the Catholic Church... Ah! wretched Protestantism shall have to answer for the loss of faith... English schism and heresy have squandered their treasures and abused their great temporal power, not only in persecuting-the faith in Great Britain and Ireland, but also in banishing the true religion of Jesus Christ from their vast American possessions ... Their long-deserved punishment, however, is approaching from the North![214]

So, at least one respected Roman priest published that a northern power will punish Britain, and its descendants, including the U.S.A. and Canada, for their "pride" and Protestantism.

But why would God allow some of these nations to be destroyed, given that the Anglo-Saxon-Americans have been in the forefront of distributing Bibles, helping in humanitarian matters, assisting with international disasters, etc.?

Partially because of their rebellion against His ways (Hosea 13:16) and lack of repentance (Hosea 11:3-5). And because:

150

⁴⁸ For everyone to whom much is given, from him much will be required (Luke 12:48).

Consider the following about American society in 2021:

> Never before in our lifetime have we seen such an abundance of widespread corruption, treacherous behavior, and blatant hypocrisy within our government. Its ruling mandate has now become, "Do as I say, not as I do". ²¹⁵

The Bible also teaches that the Assyrians will be used to punish "an hypocritical nation" (or hypocritical people, as the Hebrew can be translated) that refuses to repent:

> ⁵ O Assyrian, the rod of mine anger, and the staff in their hand is mine indignation. ⁶ I will send him against an hypocritical nation (Isaiah 10:5–6, KJV).

> ⁵ … But the Assyrian shall be his king, Because they refused to repent. (Hosea 11:5)

Christians all need to recall that when Jesus came, He clearly condemned the hypocritical religious leaders of His day (e.g. Luke 11:44), more directly than he condemned the physically more obvious sinners (Matthew 9:10–13).

This is not to say that non-Anglo-Saxon nations do not have sin or that they will not be punished. The European Assyrians will clearly also be punished, per Isaiah 10:12-19, but the **punishment will begin first** on those who should have known better. That is, the punishment will begin on those who have claimed to live rightly, but have repeatedly failed to do so. Those who receive biblical blessing should not be surprised when they receive biblical curses for disobedience (cf. Deuteronomy 28:1-68).

While the gospel warning message will be made fairly clear to the English-speaking peoples by the "Philadelphia Christians," prior to Daniel 11:39, because the Anglo-American nations are not likely to heed that warning, they will have to answer for their relative lack of response (cf. Ezekiel 33:7-9) and their survivors will be taken captive (cf. Habakkuk 2:7).

Notice something from the Sibylline oracle, followed by a comment by one who translated the passages:

> But then as time rolled around there rose the Egyptian kingdom, then … of Assyria and Babylon …
>
> For he who rules in heaven completed earth To be a common property for all, And in all bosoms placed he noblest thought. To them alone the bounteous field yields fruit, A hundred-fold from one, and thus completes God's measure. But to them shall also come misfortune, nor will they escape all plague.
>
> And even thou, forsaking thy fair shrine, Shalt flee away when it becomes thy lot to leave the holy ground, and thou shalt be carried to the Assyrians, and shalt see Wives and young children serving hostile men.
>
> Comment by *Milton Spenser Terry* (19th century): *Assyrians.* — Assyria and Babylon seem to have been often confounded together by the Sibylline authors.[216]

Thus, even the Sibyl may be warning that some who received God's blessings will be taken away and held captive by the Assyrians, who have a relationship with Babylon. This seems to be consistent with biblical prophecies, such as several in Revelation 17. Although some may feel this has been fulfilled (and perhaps in antetype it partially was), according to the Bible, it will happen in the future.

More about Verse 39

If the Great Monarch is the King of the North, then the many ruled over in Daniel 11:39 would seem to be those in the U.S., United Kingdom, Canada, Australia, and New Zealand.

Furthermore, the dividing of the land of the United States, etc., for gain, will in no small way help prosper the King of the North's empire. Many others may assist in this attack outside of those in Psalm 83. Mexico, who wants its lost land back, comes to mind.

Because of U.S.A. debts, a Russian professor named Igor Panarin has predicted that the Europeans, Russians, Mexicans, and Asians may divide the land of the U.S.A. in the 21st century.[217] And a Roman Catholic prophecy (previously cited[218]) shows that the U.K. will be divided.

China and the Land Prophecy

There is also an ancient Chinese prophecy that hints that areas like Australia and/or New Zealand could end up as part of China.[219] The Chinese, in reaction to a deal made by Australian Prime Minister Julia Gillard and Barack Obama, indicated that this and the expanded military cooperation between Australia and the U.S.A. is putting Australia at risk of attack by China.[220]

China may be granted lands like Australia in partial repayment for the debts that the U.S.A. owes it, as well as in full payment for any debts Europe itself may incur with

China (it is likely that China will loan money and/or increase investments in Europe).

It is also possible that a country like Japan may get some Anglo-Saxon dominated land (New Zealand comes to mind) in partial repayment for the debts that the U.S.A. owes it (and also possibly Europe) since the King of the North will divide land for gain.

Perhaps it should also be mentioned that the dividing of the conquered lands also seems to be foretold in the Bible in Lamentations 4:16 and Joel 3:2.

Destruction is Coming

Yet, instead of being worried about this coming Beast power, the U.S.A. and some of the other Anglo-Saxon powers, seem to be encouraging the development of a major power in Europe.[221] This is something that the Anglo-Saxon-American peoples will come to later regret.

Unless the English-speaking peoples soon repent of their sins, which is very unlikely, the Bible indicates that their nations will be destroyed relatively soon (see also Hosea 8:1-13).

The Roman Catholics also have this prophecy:

> *Balthassar Mas* (17th century): I saw a land swallowed up by the sea and covered with water. But afterwards, I saw that the sea receded little by little and the land could be seen again. The tops of the towers in the city rose again above the water and appeared more beautiful than before, and I was told that this land was England.[222]

The above may have several interpretations. Figuratively, it may mean that Protestant England is to be destroyed and will become "Catholic." Or it may simply mean some type of tsunami will affect England (it probably is not related to the prophecy in Revelation about islands, as Revelation 16:20 discusses all islands, whereas this prophecy is specific to England).

Also notice this Roman Catholic prophecy:

> *Venerable Bartholomew Holzhauser* (died 1658): England shall suffer much. The king shall be killed. After desolation has reached its peak in England peace will be restored and England will return to the Catholic faith with greater fervor than before. The Great Monarch will have the special help from God and be unconquerable.[223]

The Bible shows that the Beast will have special help from "unclean spirits" (Revelation 16:13), NOT God, and will be considered to be unconquerable (Revelation 13:4).

Notice more of what the Bible says about this:

> [3]...And all the world marveled and followed the beast. [4] So they worshiped the dragon who gave authority to the beast; and they worshiped the beast, saying, "Who is like the beast? Who is able to make war with him?" (Revelation 13:3-4)

Notice that the military power of the Beast was something that the world will marvel, be astonished about.

Why?

Because despite fascination with war (Daniel 11:38), no one truly thought that the European Beast power had the military ability to defeat the U.S.A. with its Anglo-allies

(Daniel 11:39), and then the Islamic King of the South (Daniel 11:40-43). Revelation 13:3-4 also supports the idea that the Beast may rise up because of violent civil unrest in Europe.

How can Europe rise up?

Technology appears to be the key to a powerful European military. One aspect could include particle collider research. The number of colliders in the U.S.A. dwindled down to one under the Obama and Bush Administrations.[224]

Yet, in Europe, it now has the leading one in the world, CERN's Large Hadron Collider (LHC) and Germany announced that it is planning a possibly even more advanced one called FAIR (F.A.I.R. stands for the **F**acility for **A**ntiproton and **I**on **R**esearch).[225] 3000 scientists are reportedly involved.[226] The FAIR project is in process of construction and is expected to provide beams to the experiments from 2018 onwards. PESCO is involved in numerous technological projects.

I believe that Germany's FAIR, along with the LHC and other technology like the stellarator, will help the Europeans produce military weaponry to fulfill certain end-time prophecies. Since Revelation 13:4 is discussing what seems to be a unique type of warfare, this warfare likely includes certain high-tech weapons (such as electromagnetic pulse, neutron bombs, unique delivery systems, etc.) that will be effective for a while. The FAIR and the LHC projects are also likely to spin-off economic benefits that may help propel Europe to be (for a short while) the economic leader of the world (cf. Revelation 18). Ultimately, the Europeans will be overcome by what appears to be a Russian-led, mainly Asian, confederation, cf. Jeremiah 50:41-43 & Daniel 11:44, possibly by exploiting some technological flaw, like creating a software virus, etc., while also amassing troops, etc.

The European Space Agency and other European programs related to technology like *Horizon 2020* are expected to bear fruit to the economic and military power of Europe shortly.[227] Many projects are ongoing that will assist Europe.

Germany's stellarator nuclear fusion project and Europe's Galileo satellite system are two such projects that are starting to show a lot of potential to aid the rise of Europe in the next several years.

While the U.S.A., Australia, and others are currently worried mostly about China, the European developments will end up not being good for the Anglo-Saxon descended lands, including England.

Here is one of Nostradamus' prophecies involving Germany and England:

> *Nostradamus* (died 1566) Although nations talk peace, troubles brew everywhere. Militaristic parties rise in Germany and pagan cults revive. Opinions are not free and the people are not enriched. The heir to the London government is overthrown for having made too many peace protests.[228]

While many may believe that World War II fulfilled the above, it looks a bit more likely to be related to the next war as "opinions" are less free now than they were several decades ago—and "the heir to the London government" was not truly overthrown during WWII.

Thus, both biblical and certain Roman Catholic prophecies seem to point to the destruction of the English-speaking peoples by a Great Monarch.

If you are in the Anglo-Saxon-American countries (because you did not flee with "the secret sect" of the "Nazarene" Philadelphian Christians), and you see them destroyed, will you repent then? If not, what will it take for you to do that? If you are in the Arabic lands, will you repent then, or will you wait until your great leader is destroyed shortly thereafter (Daniel 11:40-43)?

If you are elsewhere in the world, will you repent then? If not, how much will it take for you to understand these events are truly coming to pass?

Who is the Foreign God?

Notice that verse 39 also mentions a "foreign god" that the King of the North will acknowledge, and advance its glory. What god might that be?

It is remotely possible that the "foreign god" in Daniel 11:39 could be some new-age god that he, the King of the North, believes in—such as one in which demons provide him with certain direct assistance. But more likely, this god will simply be something acceptable to the new ecumenical "Catholicism" that the King of the North will publicly promote and acknowledge.

This "new religion" will have some type of image associated with it that people will be told to worship:

> [15] He was granted power to give breath to the image of the beast, that the image of the beast should both speak and cause as many as would not worship the image of the beast to be killed (Revelation 13:15).

The idea of this being a new religious order claiming to be within Roman Catholicism fits verses 38 & 39 by allowing two "gods" in a manner that would not be totally alien to some Roman Catholic practice (there have historically been many religious orders, as well as many different types of statues/icons, within Roman Catholicism).

Various Greco-Roman Catholic writers have suggested, some type of cross might be associated with this religion, its leader, and/or its image. For example, even though the Bible warns against one coming with signs and wonders (2 Thessalonians 2:8-9), an Eastern Orthodox prophecy teaches about the "Great Monarch":

> *Anonymou Paraphrasis* (10th century): The one true King...is destined to become manifest [be revealed] ... by means ... of signs... The King will hear the voice and instructions by an Angel appearing to him...he has foresight and is cognizant of the text of the prophecies...the name of the King is hidden [concealed] among the nations ... And the particular manner of the king's manifestation to the public [to the world] will take place as follows: A star will appear for three days ... And a herald speaking with a very loud voice in the course of the three days will summon and unveil the hoped for one...There will become visible in the sky a 'nebulous firmament of the sun' ... under that image will be suspended a cross ... And the invisible herald from Heaven with his thunderous voice will say to the people: Is this man agreeable to you? At that moment everybody will be taken by fear and terror.[229]

This is interesting, as some versions of crosses have long been used in other religious traditions such as Hinduism, Buddhism, and Jainism. Here is one related reference:

> [W]e find, in India, the cross bearing the same meaning as in Egypt. When with four equal arms it signifies the four elements, which cross the Hindoos

consider as eternal, and the component parts with a cross upon his breast. The cross is also found in the hands of Siva, Brahma, Vishnu, and Tvashtri...To this day, in Northern India, the cross is used to mark the jars of sacred water taken from the Indus and Ganges, as in the northeastern parts of Africa the women impress this sign as a mark of possession upon their vessels of grain, etc. In Southern India the cross is used as an emblem of disembodied Jaina saints. The worshippers of Brahma and Buddha outnumber those of Christ; and the symbol, identified as that of our Master, was revered by the East Indians—their Lao Tse, centuries before our Lord appeared upon earth.[230]

I personally have seen Hindu and Buddhist temples with crosses of various types, and have noticed that large crosses are sometimes built within them. The Angkor Wat temple in Cambodia, to cite one specific example, has several. An ecumenical cross has been promoted in recent years.[231]

Hence, Islam notwithstanding, the cross seems to be an international religious symbol. Furthermore, a symbol with a cross and crescent was used for an interfaith conference between the Vatican and certain Muslims.[232]

Thus, because the bulk of the world will tend to accept this religion (Revelation 13:3-4,8), some type of ecumenical religious order, possibly using some type of a cross as a symbol, would seem to appeal to "foreigners" of all types. Thus, this may be what the "foreign god" will represent.
As Islam is opposed to icons, and especially any type of cross as a symbol (the Crusaders, "cross bearers" invaded them centuries ago), Muslims will likely strongly question where all of this is leading.

Once the U.S.A. and its Anglo-Saxon allies are out of the way, the King of the North will likely declare that a new world order of peace has been ushered in. That is consistent with Jeremiah 6:14–15a, which is a warning about peace statements from one associated with abomination.

An ancient Chinese prophecy states:

> Beautiful people come from the West. Korea, China and Japan are gradually at peace.[233]

This prophecy seems to indicate that many Asians will accept a type of peace that will be related to a Western (European) power.

In the 19th century, someone claimed, "if you tell a lie often enough, the people will ultimately believe it."[234] Many will believe that it is a time of peace around then, but some will correctly doubt it.

The distrust of the proclamations by the "crusaders," combined with the prevalence of crosses being displayed, may be part of what triggers the prophesied attack from the Islamic King of the South.

40 "At the time of the end the king of the South shall attack him; and the king of the North shall come against him like a whirlwind, with chariots, horsemen, and with many ships; and he shall enter the countries, overwhelm them, and pass through."

The one called the King of the South in the above passage may be one with the title "Mahdi" and/or "Caliph." While Shi'ites (and some other Muslims) consider that he will be "a saviour" and establish an Islamic world, the Bible clearly shows that the King of the North will defeat him (see also Daniel 11:41-43). Hence, all Muslims need to be on their guard and *not* accept any pan-Islamic militaristic leader — especially one who looks to rise up in this decade. He will not be God's representative, and he will lose.

Presuming that the republic of the U.S.A. and its Anglo-Saxon allies are taken over in verse 39, there are several reasons why the King of the South may decide to launch his major attack shortly thereafter:

> 1) The fact that "the Great Satan," a term that certain Muslims call the U.S.A., has been eliminated, the King of the South will realize that the deals made (Daniel 11:27; Psalm 83) with the Assyrian King of the North are of little or no value anymore.

> 2) Next, without the nominally Protestant U.S.A. in its way, the King of the North will try to impose its non-Muslim religion on more and more of the world. As many Arabs tend to be more devoutly religious than the Chinese and Russians, they would be more likely to get upset with this before the Kings of the East and North-East (which occurs in Daniel 11:44).

> 3) Because the Arab confederation wanted to eliminate Israel (Psalm 83 most likely refers to the nation of Israel as well as the U.S.A. and any other serious Israeli allies), it probably will think that its actions greatly helped the Europeans accomplish this. Because of this thinking, the King of the South may become emboldened.

> 4) While the Bible shows that Europe will get a "great army," it shows that the King of the South will be in charge of "a very great and mighty army" (Daniel 11:25). This will likely give the King of the South misplaced confidence to attack. Yet, it seems

likely that it will be European military technology that will allow it to defeat the seemingly larger army that the King of the South leads.

5) It is also likely that the King of the South will feel that the conquest of the U.S.A. and its final allies will strain the military of the King of the North. The King of the South may believe it is an ideal time to strike. This is likely, as one of the reasons that the U.S.A. may be so easy to take over is because its own military has been strained, given that the U.S.A. has been spreading its military strength quite thin in the 21st century (and defense cuts have been proposed and some implemented).

6) Increasing displays of crosses, combined with people following wonders, perhaps including apparitions claiming to be Mary (see also the book *Fatima Shock!*), will get many in the Arab lands to remember the crusades. Enough will apparently hold to some version of Islam that they will fear an attack must be made or Islam will be defeated.

7) Finally, as many of the Arab economies are dependent upon oil revenues, and many oil fields may have passed their halfway point of production by that stage (and many of its weapons will be of Anglo-Saxon-American origins) while the West pushes other energy sources, the King of the South may decide that there is no better time to attack.

Also note that verse 40 says this attack against the King of the South occurs "at the time of the end." Thus, even if this had some fulfillment with Benito Mussolini or previous leaders, as has been suggested, it also has a future final fulfillment at the end.

Although the King of the North is also not "a savior" for "Catholics," notice what a Roman Catholic prophecy states:

> *Rudolph Gekner* (died 1675): **A great prince of the North with a most powerful army will traverse all Europe, uproot all republics, and exterminate all rebels.** His sword moved by Divine power will most valiantly defend the Church of Jesus Christ. He will combat on behalf of the true orthodox faith, and shall subdue to his dominion the Mahometan Empire. A new pastor of the universal church will come from the shore (of Dalmatia) through a celestial prodigy, and in simplicity of heart adorned with the doctrines of Jesus Christ. Peace will come to the world.[235]

If the above has a lot of accuracy (and it has certain biblical consistency), it seems to also show that all (or at least some) republics are to be uprooted before the Muslim King of the South is invaded.

And here are three similar, possibly related, private prophecies (the first is from a Syriac document):

> *Pseudo-Methodius* (7th century): This new Muslim invasion will be a punishment without limit and mercy...In France, people of Christians will fight and kill them...At that same time the Muslims will be killed and they will know the tribulation...The Lord will give them to the powers of the Christians whose empire will be elevated above all empires...The Roman King (Great Monarch) will show a great indignation against those who will have denied Christ in Egypt or in Arabia.[236]

Anonymou Paraphrasis (10th century): However, in the End Times…this King…will march to fight against the Ishmaelites.* And he will conquer them…[237]

St. Francis de Paul (1470):…From your lordship shall be born the great leader of the holy militia…These devout men shall wear on their breasts, and much more in their hearts, the sign of the living God, namely the cross…members of this holy order……the Great Monarch…will destroy the Mahometan sect and the rest of the infidels.[238]

(* Note the term *Ishmaelites* is a term that has been used by the Catholics and Eastern Orthodox to describe Arabs, but also has been used by them to mean all Muslims.[239])

Many "Catholics" will apparently be so misled by these and similar prophecies that they will not recognize that the "great prince of the North" seems to fulfill Daniel 11:40.

Those who profess Roman Catholicism may wish to consider what their saint Jerome taught about Daniel 11:40–43:

> …those of our viewpoint refer these details also to the Antichrist, asserting that he shall first fight against the king of the South, or Egypt, and shall afterwards conquer Libya and Ethiopia.[240]

Hence, the idea that it is an evil power that will invade the Middle East is an older tradition than the private prophecies that some may become misled into believing.

This response from the King of the North against the King of the South will effectively eliminate much called Islam.

One more verse should be perhaps touched on here, and that is Daniel 11:43.

43 He shall have power over the treasures of gold and silver, and over all the precious things of Egypt; also the Libyans and Ethiopians *shall follow* **at his heels.**

The "he" is the King of the North. This is the same King of the North that valued gold and silver in Daniel 11:38. Although other scriptures also show that gold and silver will have value around this time (like Revelation 18; 9:20), the Bible is clear that gold and silver will be worthless for a short time before Jesus returns, e.g. Ezekiel 7:19.

The fact that the King of the North himself will accumulate gold (and some silver) is consistent with several Byzantine ("Greek" Orthodox) prophecies of their expected Great Monarch:

> *Emperor Leo the Philosopher* (died 912): You will amass gold … And you will be the leader of the surrounding nations …
>
> *Addressed to Emperor Manuel II, Palaeogous* (died 1425): The Emperor … will discover gold and silver…
>
> *Saint Andrew Fool-for-Christ* (c. 4th century): God will reveal to this king all the gold wherever it happen to lay concealed from view …[241]

One side note is that, in Egypt, major gold deposits were found in 2006.[242] This is relevant as it does suggest that Egypt now has enough gold that a foreign power could be interested in taking/using it as Bible prophecy teaches.

Since many are now questioning the role of the U.S. dollar as the world's reserve currency, more are looking into other currencies as well as gold. Gold will set records in U.S. dollar terms. In 2017, I also published that in my book related to Donald Trump, and it did hit records in July and August in 2020. [243]

It has been proposed that various nations around the world are already in the process of accumulating gold to one day overthrow the U.S. dollar — and that the "U.S. is unprepared for this strategic alternative to dollar dominance."[244]

When the U.S. dollar totally collapses people all around the world will consider that even if the Euro (or something similar) is strong, having a more gold-backed currency would be safer.

The collapse of the U.S.A. dollar will shake a lot of the world's confidence in non-gold backed currencies.
The Europeans do not have to have a perfect currency, only one that is perceived to be in better shape than the U.S.A. dollar.

Having the European power acquiring more gold to back the Euro or possibly another future European currency (that might potentially replace the Euro or even a basket of currencies) may greatly increase European credibility, prosperity, and influence around the globe, even if the backing is only implied.

The debt accumulation policies of the Obama-Biden and the Trump-Pence Administrations, which were a massive acceleration of the previous policies of the Bush Administration, look like they will be continued by a Biden-Harris Administration.

The increases in America's debt are heading the world into the time when something other than the U.S. dollar will be valued as its reserve currency.

A Biden-Harris Administration would need to make massive changes to possibly prevent this.

The U.S.A. and its dollar are at serious risk.

11. Biden-Harris Will Help Fulfill End-Time Prophecies

In several ways, Joe Biden and Kamala Harris are apocalyptic leaders (cf. 2 Timothy 3:1-5). Although neither one is the final Antichrist that the Bible warns about, they look to be helping fulfill many aspects of prophecy. One or both of them are expected to help enable the rise of the final Antichrist — so will any possible successor to them.

Joe Biden has supported Islamic goals for an Arabic-confederation indirectly, and sometimes more directly, which will lead to a leader rising up over certain Islamic lands (Daniel 11:40; Ezekiel 30:1-8).

While I believe that he believes he wants to help, certain of his actions are pointing to destruction.

Presuming that the great tribulation begins (Matthew 24:21-22) 3 ½ years before the end of the 6,000 years, then the 6,000 years would be up before January 19, 2029, the end of the second presidential term from now. The destruction of the U.S.A. is coming soon. Expect that the Biden-Harris Administration will, therefore, take actions that will lead to it.

The further reality is that Joe Biden has made political, economic, and military statements which will ultimately help the rise of the upcoming Beast power in Europe. Joe Biden and Kamala Harris seem to think the relationship between Europe and the U.S.A. is better than it really is.

This European Beast power will, after it has a prophesied reorganization and rises up, destroy the United States (Daniel 11:39). And the leader of this power is supposed to rise up "When the transgressors have reached their fullness," (Daniel 8:23).

Both Joe Biden and Kamala Harris have specifically caused people of the United States to err further away from biblical morality, which will lead to destruction (Isaiah 3:12; 9:16). Instead of advocating what should be considered as biblical morality, they have pushed positions that are clearly opposed to the laws of God (e.g. Romans 1:18-32).

They have advocated policies (as have others) which are expected to increase the debt of the U.S.A., hurt its military superiority, lead to civil unrest (cf. Deuteronomy 32:25), and set the U.S.A. up for ruin (Habakkuk 2:6-8).

The Republican/Democrat Party is Not the Answer

Despite certain misunderstandings of prophecy on the Internet, the Bible IS NOT predicting that any Republican, or Democrat for that matter, will save the U.S.A. while riding a white horse (supposedly based on Revelation 6:2; 19:11-16).

The Bible says Jesus will save the world when He establishes the Kingdom of God (2 Timothy 4:1; 1 Corinthians 15:24, 50). Otherwise all flesh would be destroyed (Matthew 24:22).

Notice something from the Old Testament:

> [19] For the Lord brought Judah low because of Ahaz king of Israel, for he had encouraged moral decline in Judah and had been continually unfaithful to the Lord. (2 Chronicles 28:19)

Might leaders, like Joe Biden and Kamala Harris, who seem to be encouraging biblically-moral declines cause the U.S.A. to be brought low?

The destruction of the nation of the United States of America is coming.

As too, is the destruction of its allies the United Kingdom, Canada, Australia, and New Zealand. The U.S. president(s) during this decade will take steps which will lead to that.

"Scripture cannot be broken" (John 10:35). The biblical prophecies outlined in this book will come to pass.

While national repentance for the U.S.A. seems unlikely (Hosea 11:5), personal repentance is possible (1 Timothy 2:4; Acts 2:38). Even physical protection is available for Philadelphian Christians (cf. Revelation 3:7-10; Revelation 12:14-16).

The U.S.A. needs national repentance to delay its coming destruction (cf. Daniel 4:27).

Pray (1 Timothy 2:1-3; Matthew 6:9-13; Colossians 4:2). You do not have to have happen to you what will happen to the unrepentant U.S.A. (Luke 21:36).

Those who consider themselves Christians should heed Jesus' and the Apostle Paul's admonitions to watch world events (Mark 13:33-36; 1 Thessalonians 5:3-6) and pray to be accounted worthy to escape various events that are certain to come to pass (Luke 21:36).

Despise not prophecies (1 Thessalonians 5:20).

Endnote Citations

1 Dickenson JR. BIDEN ACADEMIC CLAIMS 'INACCURATE.' Washington Post, September 22, 1987

2 Ibid

3 Joe Biden Biography. Biography.com, accessed 12/15/20

4 Associated Press. Timeline of Biden's life and career. San Francisco Chronicle, August 23, 2008

5 Joe Biden Biography. Biography.com, accessed 12/15/20

6 Joe Biden Biography. Biography.com, accessed 12/15/20

7 Joe Biden Biography. Biography.com, accessed 12/15/20

8 Ecumenical Patriarch to Biden: Citizens of the whole free world welcome your victory. Orthodox Times, November 10, 2020

9 Callahan M. 'Gropey Uncle' Joe Biden has always been creepy and should stay out of 2020 race. NY Post, April 1, 2019

10 CNN's Stelter Slams Coverage of Hunter Biden Scandal As CNN... Press Aggregate, December 15, 2020

11 Milton J. Britain under Trojan, Roman, Saxon Rule. By John Milton.-England under Richard III. By Sir T. More.-The reign of Henry VII. By F. Bacon ... Verbatim reprint from Kennet's England, Ed. 1719. A. Murray & Son, 1870, pp. 74-75

12 Cowley A, Jacobs J, Huxley HM. Samaritans. Jewish Encyclopedia, Volume 10. Funk and Wagnalls, 1996, pp. 669-681

13 Davidiy Y. The Tribes, 4th edition. Russell-David Publishers, 2011, p. 384; Allen JH. Jacob's Sceptre and Joseph's Birthright, 19th edition. Destiny Publishers, 1902, pp. 315-317

14 Davidiy, p. 424-426

15 Davidiy, pp. 384, 445-447

16 Allen, p.315-327; Knox RT. Josephs Land: Ephriam, Or Great Britain, Manasseh Or United States, 1886. Nickels R. History of the Seventh Day Church of God. Giving & Sharing, 1994, pp. 76,142; Armstrong HW. The United States and the British Commonwealth in Prophecy. 1954; McNair R. America and Britain in Prophecy. Global Church of God, 1996, pp. 29-32; Davidiy, pp. 361-450

17 Strong's Exhaustive Concordance word #1285

18 Strong's Exhaustive Concordance word #377

19 Bowden E. Inside Joe Biden's history of falsely claiming he predicted 9/11 attacks. NY Post, September 10, 2020

20 'The Isaiah 9:10 Judgment': U.S. in crosshairs. WND, February 20, 2012

21 US Marks 9-11 Anniversary. Voice of America, September 10, 2010

22 'The Isaiah 9:10 Judgment': U.S. in crosshairs. WND, February 2012

23 Traub J. Joe Biden Is Actually Listening. ForeignPolicy.com, September 14, 2020

24 Kaczynski A. The Many Occasions Joe Biden Took Credit For Writing The Patriot Act. Buzz Feed News, September 10, 2015

25 Ibid

26 Thomas K, Siddiqui S. Biden Says Rioters Who Stormed Capitol Were Domestic Terrorists. Wall Street Journal, January 7, 2021

27 The Biden Plan to Advance LGBTQ+ Equality in America and Around the World. JoeBiden.com accessed 10/16/20

28 The Biden Emergency Action Plan to Save the Economy. JoeBiden.com, accessed 12/16/20

29 Bowden E, et al. Trump says Pelosi's 25th Amendment bill is about replacing Biden with Harris. NY Post, October 9, 2020

30 Kim C, Stanton Z. 55 Things You Need to Know About Kamala Harris. Politico, August 11, 2020

31 Devi. Antcient History Encyclopedia. AncientHistory.eu accessed 12/16/20

32 Kamala Harris Biography. Biography.com, accessed 12/16/20

33 Caldera C. Fact check: True claim about Harris failing bar exam on first try and Barrett's law school rank. USA Today, October 18, 2020

34 Kim C, Stanton Z. 55 Things You Need to Know About Kamala Harris. Politico, August 11, 2020

35 Fact check: Kamala Harris and Willie Brown had a relationship over a decade after he separated from wife. Reuters, October 13, 2020

36 Costly D. Roseanne Barr says Kamala Harris 'slept her way to the bottom'. SF Gate, March 3, 2019

37 Kamala Harris Biography. Biography.com, accessed 12/16/20

38 Kamala Harris Biography. Biography.com, accessed 12/16/20

39 Harris K. The Truths We Hold: An American Journey. Penguin Press, 2019, p. 16

40 Golden DC. Was Kamala just caught stealing a childhood story about 'Fweedom' from MLK? World Net Daily, January 5, 2021

41 Schor E. Harris brings Baptist, interfaith roots to Democratic ticket. Associated Press, August 11, 2020

42 The Biden Plan to Build Back Better by Advancing Racial Equity Across the American Economy. JoeBiden.com accessed 10/16/20

43 The Biden Plan to Build Back Better by Advancing Racial Equity Across the American Economy. JoeBiden.com accessed 01/01/21

44 McDermott P. Voices of a White Awakening. The Unz Review, December 25, 2020

45 Thiel B. Donald Trump and America's Apocalypse. Nazarene Books, 2017

46 The Biden Agenda for Women. JoeBiden.com accessed 10/16/20

47 Pro-life leaders react to Biden's 'extreme' HHS pick. Catholic News Agency, December 7, 2020

48 Kamala Harris Takes Extreme Stance on Abortion. NewsMax, August 12, 2020

49 The Biden Plan to Advance LGBTQ+ Equality in America and Around the World. JoeBiden.com accessed 10/16/20

50 The Biden Agenda for Women. JoeBiden.com accessed 10/16/20

51 Nelson S. Joe Biden transition official wrote op-ed advocating free speech restrictions. USA Today, November 13, 2020

52 Unrue B. Franklin Graham: U.S. sins 'are a stench in the nostrils of our Creator'. World Net Daily, January 6, 2021

53 IPCC Fifth Assessment Synthesis Report. CLIMATE CHANGE 2014 SYNTHESIS REPORT Longer report Adopted 1 November 2014; Europe set to Sizzle Again as Heatwave Continues. Voice of America, June 29, 2019; Beradelli J. Wildfires and weather extremes: It's not coincidence, it's climate change. CBS, September 17, 2020

54 Flynn T, Flynn M. The Thunder of Justice. MaxKol Communications, Inc. Sterling (VA), 1993,, pp. 341,342

55 Rugaber C, Madhani A. Biden names liberal econ team as pandemic threatens workers. AP, December 1, 2020

56 Krieg G, et al. Biden readies major stimulus push and flurry of executive actions in first 100 days. CNN, December 1, 2020

57 Stein J, et al. Biden assembling new stimulus plan with checks, unemployment aid. Washington Post, January 8, 2021

58 Rickards J. Axis of Gold. The Daily Reckoning, December 20, 2016

59 Ibid

60 Gertz B, China Debt Threat. Washington Times, March 2, 2011

61 Escobar P. BRICS was created as a tool of attack: Lula. Asia Times, August 28, 2019

62 Conway E. Britain showing signs of heading towards 1930s-style depression, says Bank. Telegraph, March 16, 2009

63 Snyder M. As Yellowstone Awakens, Dr. Michio Kaku Warns That It Could "Literally Tear The Guts Out Of The United States Of America". Economic Collapse Blog, February 2019

64 Germany Calls Allegations of US Bugging 'Unacceptable.' VOA, July 1, 2013

65 Rehle M. U.S. taps half-billion German phone, internet links in month: report. Reuters, June 30, 2014

66 Rehle M. U.S. taps half-billion German phone, internet links in month: report. Reuters, June 30, 2014

67 Heilbrunn J. The German-American breakup. Los Angeles Times, July 10, 2014

68 Ukraine crisis: Transcript of leaked Nuland-Pyatt call. BBC News, February 7, 2014

69 Biden to name Sherman, Nuland to top diplomatic posts: sources. Reuters, January 5, 2021

70 Gardiner N. European Union army is not in America's interests. Washington Times, October 31, 2016

71 Germans consider US as reliable a partner as Russia – poll. RT, February 4, 2017

72 Trump worries Nato with 'obsolete' comment. BBC, Janaury 16, 2017

73 Trump defence chief Mattis threatens less commitment to Nato. January 15, 2017; Sanger DE, Haberman M. Donald Trump Sets Conditions for Defending NATO Allies Against Attack. New York Times, July 20, 2016

74 Europe hates Trump. Does it matter? BBC, March 4, 2016

75 Wish List or Reality? Digital Trends in 2016 | Karl-Theodor zu Guttenberg | hub conference. https://www.youtube.com/watch?v=dgdZUA96UBU. Posted 12/11/ 2015

76 Stur B. The making of a European Defence Union. New Europe. December 12, 2017

77 Bosotti A. EU army plot to fuel 'antagonistic' fury from global enemies and spark conflict threat. December 1, 2020; Flores J. The End of NATO? Macron Laments 'Brain Death' and Pushes for a European Military. Strategic Culture, November 10, 2019

78 Walt V. 'Trump Has Been a Kind of Awakening.' E.U's Top Diplomat Says Europe's Relationship With U.S. Is Forever Changed. Time, November 17, 2020

79 Alden C. China and Europe Won't Get Any Relief on Trade From Biden. ForeignPolicy.com, November 6, 2020

80 Cunningham F. Trust in American Politics Has Tanked… and That Means War. Strategic Culture, January 5, 2021

81 Russia Is 'Deeply European,' France's Macron Says in Russian. The Moscow Times, August 20, 2019

82 Kurbjuweit D. America Has Abdicated Its Leadership of the West. Spiegel Online, November 16, 2016

83 Karnitschnig M. Why Europe secretly roots for Donald Trump. Strategic-Culture.org. September 22, 2016

84 Air Force Official Disputes GAO Report on Projected GPS Failure. Satellite Today, May 26, 2009

85 Thiel B. 2012 and the Rise of the Secret Sect. Nazarene Books, 2009, p. 89

86 Butler A. U.S. Satellite Coverage Gaps Loom. Aviation Week, November 10, 2009

87 As quoted in: North R. Galileo: The Military and Political Dimensions, Paper no. 47. Bruggesgroup.com accessed 12/29/16

88 Amos J. EU awards Galileo satellite-navigation contracts. BBC, Jan 7, 2010

89 A Wolfowitz P. Letter to the Honorable Minster of Defense. Office of the US Deputy Secretary of Defense, December 2, 2001

90 Wolf J. US, wary of China, mulls satellite substitutes. Reuters, February 4, 2010

91 U.S. and the EU to collaborate on usage of Global Navigation Satellite Systems. BNO News, July 31, 2010

92 Stearns S. Kerry: US to Work Closely With Allies Over Surveillance Concerns. VOA, November 5, 2013

93 US 'Muslim ban' set to end 'on day one' of Biden presidency. Aljazeera, November 8, 2020

94 Hennessey K. Obama outlines strategy to 'ultimately destroy' Islamic State. Los Angeles Times, September 5, 2014

95 Glasse C. New Encyclopedia of Islam: A Revised Edition of the Concise Encyclopedia of Islam, 3rd edition, 2008, pp. 143, 316

96 North Thunder 'achieved more than desired results.' Arab News, March 5, 2017

97 Reagen DR. Further Thoughts About a Muslim Antichrist. Bible Prophecy Today, March 16, 2009.

98 Understanding the Muslim Brotherhood, IKWANWEB, The official website of the Muslim Brotherhood, February 14, 2011

99 Nayouf, Hayyan. Translated from Arabic by Sonia Farid. Shiite scholar denies Obama link
to Muslim savior. Dubai. November 4, 2008.
http://www.alarabiya.net/articles/2008/11/04/59490.html viewed 05/19/09

100 Erlanger S. Biden Wants to Rejoin Iran Nuclear Deal, but It Won't Be Easy ... New York Times, November 18, 2020

101 Norman L. Europe Hopeful Trump Will Stick With Iran Nuclear Deal. Wall Street Journal, December 13, 2016

102 Iran Parliament to debate bill calling for Israel's destruction by 2040. i24news, January 6, 2021

103 The Qur'an. From chapter 43 http://www.usc.edu/schools/college /crcc/engagement/resources/texts/muslim/quran/043.qmt.html 03/22/09

104 Richardson J. Antichrist: Islam's Awaited Messiah. Pleasant Word, 2006, p. 48

105 Ibn Zubair Ali, Mohammed Ali. The minor signs of Last Days from: The Signs of Qiyamah. http://www.islamawareness.net/Prophecies/minor.html viewed 08/11/12

106 Hippolytus. On Christ and Antichrist, Chapter 43

107 Irenaeus. Against Heresies, Book V, Chapter 25, verse 4

108 Moore A. Catholic archbishop: Biden 'irreparable disaster' as president. World Net Daily, January 4, 2021

109 Fung K. Conservative Pastor Robert Henderson says Kamala Harris is Driven by the "Antichrist Spirit' Newsweek, November 18, 2020

110 Eusebius. The History of the Church, Book 5, Chapter XXIV. Digireads.com, 2005, p. 115

111 Wilhelm J. Apostolic Succession. The Catholic Encyclopedia, Volume I. Copyright © 1907 by Robert Appleton Company. Nihil Obstat, March 1, 1907. Remy Lafort, S.T.D., Censor. Imprimatur. +John Cardinal Farley, Archbishop of New York

112 Pui-Hua R. Ancient Chinese Prophecies Till the End of the World. AuthorHouse, Bloomington (IN), 2008, p. 85

113 Pui-Hua, p. 89

114 Kramer H.B. L. The Book of Destiny, pp. 318,319

115 Maas, Anthony. "Antichrist." The Catholic Encyclopedia. Vol. 1. New York: Robert Appleton Company, 1907. Nihil Obstat. March 1, 1907. Remy Lafort, S.T.D., Censor. Imprimatur. +John Cardinal Farley, Archbishop of New York. 10 Dec. 2008

116 Tzima Otto, p. 138

117 Annotations on The Second Epistle of Saint Paul to the Thessalonians. The Original and True RHEIMS NEW TESTAMENT of Anno Domini 1582 , p. 423

118 Babylonian Talmud: Tractate Sanhedrin Folio 97a

119 Pirke De Rabbi Eliezer, Gerald Friedlander, Sepher-Hermon Press, New York, 1981, p. 141

120 Seligsohn M. Seder Olam. Jewish Encyclopedia of 1906; Berkowitz AE. Scientist Claims Redemption May Be Much Closer Than You Thought. Breaking Israel News, June 28, 2018; First M.Jewish History in Conflict: A Study of the Major Discrepancy between Rabbinic and Conventional Chronology, 1997

121 Eusebius. The History of the Church, Book III, Chapter XXIX, Verse 12, p. 69

122 Irenaeus. Adversus haereses, Book V, Chapter 28:2-3

123 Irenaeus. Adversus haereses, Book V, Chapter 30:4

124 St. Hippolytus of Rome, The Catholic Encyclopedia, 1910

125 Hippolytus. On the HexaËmeron, Or Six Days' Work. From Fragments from Commentaries on Various Books of Scripture

126 Rupert GG. Time, Tradition, and Truth Concerning the End of the World, 3rd edition. Union Publishing Company, 1918, pp. 26-30

127 Culligan E. The Last World War and the End of Time. The book was blessed by Pope Paul VI, 1966. TAN Books, Rockford (IL), pp. 113-115

128 Rossi, Gaudentius. The Christian Trumpet: Or, Previsions and Predictions about Impending General Calamities, the Universal Triumph of the Church, the Coming of the Anti-Christ, the Last Judgment, and the End of the World; Divided Into Three Parts, 4th edition. Patrick Donahoe, 1875, pp. 233-238

129 Cupper28. Kaliyuga Ends by 2025, Mystry. Daily English News, July 4, 2018

130 Hindu Prophecies: The Kalki Purana. viewed 12/29/20 http://www-iii.tripod.com/hindu.htm

131 Kumar, Vijay. End of the World 2012. viewed Spring 2009, http://www.godrealized.com/2012.html htm

132 Cardinal Stafford criticizes Obama as 'aggressive, disruptive and apocalyptic'. Catholic News Agency. Nov 17, 2008. http://catholicnewsagency.com/new.php?n=14355 viewed 03/01/09

133 Stafford, Cardinal James Francis. Cardinal's Address to Catholic University of America, November 13, 2008. Catholic News Agency. http://www.catholicnewsagency.com/document.php?n=780 viewed 03/01/09

134 Farm Bureau. Trump v Biden: Where do the candidates stand on GMOs and other key food issues? Genetic Literacy Project, November 17, 2020

135 Hopi Civilization. http://2012wiki.com/index.php?title=Hopi_Civilization viewed 01/14/08

136 "Visions of the Great Nyasaye, A Study of the Luo Religion in Kenya", Order of Sorcha Faal, Sister Mary McCrea © 1915; © February 13, 2008.

137 Stockbauer B. Native American prophecies, UFO's and the coming of a messiah. http://mindlight.info/maitreya/bsprophe.htm viewed 06/05/14

138 Crystal E. Hopi Prophecies. http://www.crystalinks.com/hopi2.html viewed 06/05/14

139 Huchedé, P. Translated by JBD. History of Antichrist. Imprimatur: Edward Charles Fabre, Bishop of Montreal. English edition 1884, Reprint 1976. TAN Books, Rockford (IL), p. 24

140 Dupont, p. 93

141 Dupont, p.94

142 Dupont, p. 94

143 Chopra, R. editor in chief. Nostradamus Prophecies with Famous Examples. http://www.liveindia.com/nostradamus/famous.html viewed 11/29/08

144 Nostradamus. Les Propheties. 1840 Bareste edition.

145 Agrawal S. From zombie apocalypse and global famine to meteor strike and WW3, here are Nostradamus' predictions for 2021. Times Now News, January, 1, 2021

146 Culleton R. Gerald. The Prophets and Our Times. Nihil Obstat: L. Arvin. Imprimatur: Philip G. Scher, Bishop of Monterey-Fresno, November 15, 1941 Reprint 1974, TAN Books,
Rockford (IL), pp. 177-178

147 Culleton, The Prophets and Our Times, pp. 171,172

148 Birch, DA. Trial, Tribulation & Triumph: Before During and After Antichrist. Queenship Publishing Company, Goleta (CA), 1996, pp. 225,226

149 Birch, pp. 553, 555

150 Pope's Address at Being Awarded Charlemagne Prize. Zenit, May 6, 2016

151 Wilders G. Political Revolution Is Brewing in Europe. Gatestone Institute, December 21, 2016

152 Stur B. The making of a European Defence Union. New Europe, December 12, 2017

153 Penn L. False Dawn. Sophia Perennis, 2005, p. 420

154 Thigpen P. The Rapture Trap, 2nd edition. Nihil obstat Joseph C. Price, June 14, 2002. Imprimatur Anthony Cardinal Bevilacqua, Archbishop of Philadelphia, June 18, 2002. Ascension Press, 2002, pp. 222-225

155 Jerome. Commentary on Daniel, Chapter 11. Translated by Gleason L. Archer. (1958).

156 Pay Attention to Daniel's Prophecy! Watchtower Bible and Tract Society of New York, Brooklyn, 1999; 2006 printing, p. 218

157 Pay Attention to Daniel's Prophecy!, p. 247

158 Revelation, Chapter 3. United States Conference of Catholic Bishops. www.usccb.org/bible/revelation/3 viewed 08/25/2012

159 1 Nephi 13:4-5

160 Fausset, A. R., A.M. "Commentary on Daniel 11". "Commentary Critical and Explanatory on the Whole Bible". http://bible.crosswalk.com/Commentaries/JamiesonFaussetBrown /jfb.cgi?book=da&chapter=011>. 1871. viewed 7/23/08

161 Holy Bible: Vine's Expository Reference Edition., p. 788

162 Jerome. Commentary on Daniel, Chapter 11.

163 Culleton, The Prophets and Our Times, p. 226

164 Huchedé P. History of Antichrist. Imprimatur Edward Charles Fabre, Bishop of Montreal, First English edition 1884. 1976 TAN Books, Rockford (IL), p. 22

165 Jerome. Commentary on Daniel, Chapter 11

166 Birch, pp. 317,326; Dupont, pp.60,62,71

167 Jerome. Commentary on Daniel, Chapter 11

168 Berkowitz AE. Miracle of Ingathering at Dedication of Altar for Third Temple. Breaking Israel News, December 10, 2018

169 Culleton, The Prophets and Our Times, p. 151

170 U.S. and the EU to collaborate on the usage of Global Navigation Satellite Systems. Wire Update, BNO News, July 31, 2010

171 Dupont, p.18

172 Tzima Otto, H. The Great Monarch and WWIII in Orthodox, Roman Catholic and Scriptural Prophecies. Verenikia Press, Rock Hill (SC), 2000,, p. 316

173 Connor, p. 32

174 Gigot FE. 'The Abomination of Desolation.' The Catholic Encyclopedia, Volume I. Nihil Obstat, March 1, 1907. Remy Lafort, S.T.D., Censor. Imprimatur. +John Cardinal Farley, Archbishop of New York 1907

175 The Original And True Douay Old Testament Of Anno Domini 1610, Prepared and Edited by Dr. William von Peters, Ph.D. Copyright © 2005, p. 741

176 Clarke A. The Adam Clarke Commentary, Daniel Chapter 11.

177 By Anne Emmerich, in Thiel B. 2012 and the Rise of the Secret Sect. Nazarene Books, 2009, p. 106

178 By Andrew Fool for Christ, in Tzima Otto, p. 113

179 In this Sign you will conquer with One Voice. Cyndi Cain's SYMPHONY OF SUFFERING column DailyCatholic.org September 3-5, 2001 volume 12, no. 148

180 Tzima Otto, p. 240

181 OT:6256 `eth. Biblesoft's New Exhaustive Strong's Numbers and Concordance with Expanded Greek-Hebrew Dictionary. Copyright (c) 1994, Biblesoft and International Bible Translators, Inc.

182 The Wycliffe Bible Commentary, Daniel 12:1

183 Dupont, Yves. Catholic Prophecy: The Coming Chastisement. TAN Books, Rockford (IL), 1973, p.38

184 Dupont, p.31

185 Kramer H.B. L. The Book of Destiny. Nihil Obstat: J.S. Considine, O.P., Censor Deputatus. Imprimatur: +Joseph M. Mueller, Bishop of Sioux City, Iowa, January 26, 1956. Reprint TAN Books, Rockford (IL), pp. 296-297

186 Graff, Ron and Dolphin, Lambert. Thy Kingdom Come, Thy Will Be Done..., Chapter 11. Peninsula Bible Church, Palo Alto (CA), 1998

187 LaHaye T, Hindson E. The Popular Bible Prophecy Commentary. Harvest House, Eugene (OR), 2006, pp. 523-524

188 Hildegard of Bingen. Scivias. Paulist Press, Mahwah (NJ), pp. 301-302

189 Rheims New Testament, p. 556

190 Irenaeus. Adversus haereses, Book V, Chapter 34, Verse 3. From Ante-Nicene Fathers, Volume 1. Edited by Alexander Roberts & James Donaldson. 1885

191 Hippolytus. On Christ and Antichrist, Chapter 61

192 Cyril of Jerusalem. Catechetical Lecture 15

193 Victorinus of Petau. Commentary on the Apocalpyse. Ante-Nicene Christian library:...the Fathers down to A.D. 325. T. and T. Clark, 1870, p. 423

194 Revelation, Chapter 3. United States Conference of Catholic Bishops. www.usccb.org/bible/revelation/3 viewed 08/25/2012

195 Tzima Otto, pp.190, 274

196 José Hoíl J, Roys R. The Book of Chilam Balam of Chumayel. Roys Publisher, 1933. Reprint Forgotten Books, 1967, p. 80

197 José Hoíl, p. 233

198 Ogwyn J. The United States and Great Britain in Prophecy. LCG, p. 42

199 Interlinear Transliterated Bible. Dan 11:36, 6213. Copyright (c) 1994 by Biblesoft

200 Gesenius HFW, Driver SR, Briggs CA, Brown F, Robinson E. A Hebrew and English Lexicon of the Old Testament.

201 Culligan, pp. 118-119

202 Culleton, The Prophets and Our Times, pp. 131,132

203 Culleton, The Prophets and Our Times, p. 163

204 Culleton, The Prophets and Our Times, p. 137

205 Dupont, p.15

206 Connor, p.30

207 Culleton RG. The Reign of Antichrist. Reprint TAN Books, Rockford, IL, 1974., p. 163

208 Birch, pp. 308-309

209 Kramer P. What are the missing contents of the third secret? Fatima Crusader, 95. Summer 20120, pp, 45-46

210 Connor, p. 33

211 Tzima Otto, p, 116

212 Flynn, p. A259

213 Lindsey H. The Hal Lindsey Report. Trinity Broadcasting Company, original air date May 1, 2009

214 Rossi, pp. 16, 255

215 Gendon M. God's Prophetic Word Encourages Believers. PTG Newsletter, January 1, 2021

216 The Sibylline Oracles, Book III, verses 188, 308-319, pp. 78,83

217 Osborn A. As if Things Weren't Bad Enough, Russian Professor Predicts End of U.S. Wall Street Journal, Dec 29, 2008

218 Culleton, The Reign of Antichrist, p. 163

219 Pui-Hua, p. 164. The ancient Chinese prophecy states, "Population mouth takes territories south of the Yangtze river. The capital is moved again. The two divide up the territories, of which each maintains and defends." This may be related to a deal that the Chinese could make in the future with Europe, as opposed to military conquest. It also may not be related to the taking of Australia or New Zealand, but perhaps might be.

220 Obama addresses troops at final stop in Australia. New York Times, November 17, 2011; Wen P. Chinese Official: it's us or America. National Times, May 16, 2012

221 Gardiner N. Barack Obama will back a federal Europe. Telegraph, March 18, 2009. Clinton, Hillary. America's Pacific Century. Foreign Policy, November 2011

222 Dupont, p. 32

223 Culleton, The Prophets and Our Times, p. 172

224 Matson J. Nuclear Decelerator: Last U.S. Particle Collider is on Chopping Block. Scientific American, August 24, 2012

225 JCW. Go-ahead for €1.6 billion particle accelerator. The Local, June 13, 2012

226 FAIR - An International Facility for Antiproton and Ion Research. http://www.fair-center.eu/ accessed 12/02/16

227 Horizon 2020: The EU Framework Programme for Research and Innovation. European Commission. http://ec.europa.eu/programmes/horizon2020/en/

228 Culleton, The Prophets and Our Times, p. 165

229 Tzima-Otto, pp. 30, 31, 32, 50-51, 52

230 Seymour W.W. The cross in tradition, history, and art. G.P. Putnams'sons, 1898. Original from Princeton University. Digitized Sep 19, 2008, pp. 910

231 Kenny P. Salvadoran cross that is Christian sign of unity is dedicated at Ecumenical Center in Geneva. Ecumenical News, January 18, 2018

232 Vatican releases program for Apostolic Journey to Morocco. Vatican News, January 7, 2019

233 Pui-Hua, p. 85

234 Cumming J. Sabbath evening readings on the New Testament. 1861. Original from Oxford University Digitized Aug 15, 2006, p. 234

235 Connor, p. 36

236 Araujo, Fabio R. Selected Prophecies and Prophets. BookSurge LLC, Charlestown (SC), 2007, p. 103

237 Tzima Otto, p. 32

238 Culleton, The Prophets and Our Times, p. 157-161

239 Tzima Otto, p. 178

240 Jerome. Commentary on Daniel, Chapter 11

241 Tzima Otto, pp. 76, 102, 114

242 A Gold Mine Worth LE 23 Billion (and counting). Egypt Today, August, 2006

243 Gold hits new record, posts best month since 2016 CNBC, July 30, 2020; Woodall T. Gold surges to new highs as US dollar weakens despite growing macro risks. S&P Global, August 10, 2020

244 Rickards J. Axis of Gold. The Daily Reckoning, December 20, 2016

Free Newsletter

You can get a free and essentially daily email newsletter of news events with prophetic-connections from Dr. Thiel by signing up for it at: http://www.cogwriter.com/news/

Bible News Prophecy program Videos

Dr. Thiel has online videos on several platforms:

http://www.youtube.com/BibleNewsProphecy
https://vimeo.com/channels/biblenewsprophecy
https://www.brighteon.com/channel/ccogbnp
https://www.bitchute.com/channel/prophecy/
https://www.dailymotion.com/dm_e24c8ac0050c5e7445cd5573
711869c6/videos

Internet Radio & Mobile App

Dr. Thiel is on **Bible News Prophecy** radio
http://www.biblenewsprophecy.net/
http://www.biblenewsprophecy.net/mobile-radio

Printed in Great Britain
by Amazon